Norwich
the growth of a city

Barbara Green BSc AMA FSA
Rachel M R Young MA

Norfolk Museums Service

Director Francis Cheetham OBE BA FMA

Dedicated to the memory of R. Rainbird Clarke, MA, FSA, FMA,
Curator of the Norwich Museums, 1951-1963

Cover Norwich from the south east
Oil on canvas, dated 1849
Alfred Priest (1810-1850)

© Norfolk Museums Service 1981
Revised edition ISBN 0 903101 37 8
Witley Press Ltd., Hunstanton, Norfolk

Contents

List of figures

Unless otherwise stated, the subjects of the illustrations are in the Norwich Museums' collections. All photographs are copyright of the Norfolk Museums Service unless noted otherwise

Maps

Illustrations

Foreword

In 1963, the first edition of this booklet, written by Barbara Green and Rachel Young, was published to accompany a temporary exhibition of the same name held at the Castle Museum. Since then, there has been a great deal of research into all aspects of the City's history and much of the information obtained has been incorporated into this volume with its new, illustrated format. The sources of the illustrations are given in the list of figures and our thanks must go to all those who have allowed us to use their material. Excavations have been carried out in Norwich between 1971 and 1978 by the Norwich Survey under its director Alan Carter, and from 1979 onwards by Brian Ayers for the Norfolk Archaeological Unit. These excavations have, in particular, considerably modified the earlier interpretations of the origins and growth of the Anglo-Saxon and Norman town. The sections covering these periods have been largely re-written by Barbara Green and the help and criticism of Malcolm Atkin, Brian Ayers and Alan Carter are most gratefully acknowledged. The sections covering the history of Norwich since the 17th century have been revised by Michael Day and Penny Marsh from recent research at the Bridewell Museum.

Special thanks are due to Richard Malt who was responsible for the design of this edition, Andrew Walker who re-drew the first four maps, Rachel Young for her help in the revision of the text and bibliography and Norma Watt for her help with the illustrations.

Francis Cheetham

Director, Norfolk Museums Service

The Geographical Position of Norwich

The plateau of east Norfolk is drained by four main rivers which share a common outlet at Great Yarmouth. This plateau rarely rises above 300 feet and it is generally well below that level. The plateau itself is composed of sands, gravels and clays overlying the chalk. Much of this area is drained by the rivers Yare and Wensum and their tributaries and, when most of the plateau was heavily forested, these provided routes from the coastal strip to the interior. The comparatively slight fall from the river sources to the sea and the soft nature of the rocks has meant that these meandering rivers have cut fairly broad valleys which are filled with alluvium and often edged with gravel terraces.

Norwich developed from a number of small settlements established on the well-drained gravel terraces, above the normal level of winter flooding and with easy access to an adequate water supply. It lies adjacent to the lowest ford-ing point of the river Wensum, above its confluence with the river Yare, and at a point where the gravel terraces on either side of the river approach each other most closely, providing an easy crossing from the north to the south side. The maps show quite clearly how the inhabited area from the mid 13th century to the end of the 18th century on the north side of the river, as defined by the line of the city walls, was almost entirely confined to these well-drained gravel soils. On the south side the picture is somewhat different. The westerly spread of settlement ceased at Westwick where the area of alluvium between the edge of the terrace and the river was much wider. Instead, settlement spread up the slope, where water was available from a number of small streams or cockeys. The line of the 13th century defences here is not so closely related to topographical features, but rather reflects the general western and southern limits of the inhabited areas at that period. At the foot of the steep cliff above what is now King Street, occupation was restricted to a narrow terrace and formed part of the southward spread of settle-ment. Despite the dedications of some of the churches to Saxon saints, expansion of settlement into this area seems not to have taken place until after the Norman Conquest. Archaeological evidence suggests an early 12th century date for the beginnings of settlement where the church of St. Etheldreda now stands.

The development of Norwich from a number of small riverine settlements to one of the five largest towns in England by 1065 is due to a series of geographical and historical factors which are so inter-related that it is essen-tial to consider them together. Until about the time of the birth of Christ, west Norfolk with its light, easily worked soils, was the main centre of population, but improved tools and techniques enabled farmers to clear the forest which blanketed the richer soils of the east. By the Nor-man Conquest there had been a definite shift in the centre of population from west to east, and this in terms of numbers of people was quite considerable, for Norfolk was amongst the most densely populated areas of Britain. The population was spread more evenly over the land than it is today, for the population of Norwich in 1086 was about 5,500 compared with a total population for the county of perhaps 125,000. Today, out of about 686,300 in the whole county of Norfolk, nearly a quarter (almost 180,000) are concentrated in Norwich and the built-up area surrounding it. An essential need of a predominantly agricultural population, producing more than was needed for mere subsistence, was the establishment of trading centres. The position of Norwich in the midst of this rapidly developing farming area made it an ideal centre. It lies at a focus of natural routes along the valleys of the rivers Yare and Wensum and their tributaries, and there is growing evidence that the pattern of Roman roads may have been a contributing factor as well. A development of inland ports in the Saxon period is well attested along the east coast of England and on the opposite side of the North Sea. The development of Norwich as an inland port for trade with Western Europe, before the rise of Yarmouth, was a vital factor in its growth.

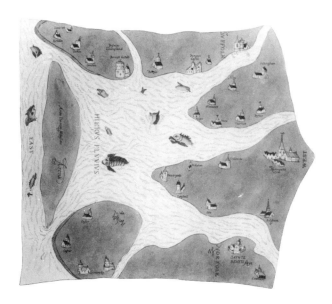

1 *A late 16th century reconstruction of east Norfolk in about* AD *1000, showing Norwich as a sea port.*

The sand spit on which Yarmouth was established had probably not developed by this time and access to the three main rivers was comparatively easy. The estuary itself was more open and the rivers broader, at least as far upstream as the tidal limit, though by the end of the Saxon period the restriction of the river valleys and the outlet to the sea would have approached the pattern familiar to us today. The development of Norwich as a port, rather than other possible sites such as Beccles, which is on the river Waveney and at the focus of routes from the west of north Suffolk, south Norfolk and the Cambridge region, is related to the nature of the trading vessels. Norwich was easily accessible to square-rigged ships, which would have been very much more difficult to take up the river Waveney. The river Yare was not navigable by sea-going vessels above its confluence with the river Wensum, while the head of navigation in the latter river has always been in the immediate area of Norwich. It was almost inevitable therefore that Norwich, so well situated to serve the needs of the population of the prosperous east and central Norfolk agricultural area as a local trading centre and continental port, should have risen to pre-eminence in the Late Saxon period and retained its position for so many centuries.

Norfolk was comparatively isolated from the Midlands by the Fens, and to travel by land was difficult until the 19th century. This, together with the ease of sea communications, has tended to strengthen Norfolk's contacts with Western Europe and provide a source of influence apparent at many periods in the history of the area.

Early Occupation

Though the potentialities of the site of Norwich were not fully exploited until the Late Saxon period, there is ample evidence for occupation of the Greater Norwich area at all periods after the Great Ice Age. Activity during the Mesolithic and Neolithic periods (about 10,000 – 2000 B.C.) is attested mainly by flint implements, which are found scattered not only in the river valleys but also on the higher ground. These indicate some arable farming in the Neolithic period, for the principal use of flint axes was for clearing woodland to make small plots for cultivation. Low-lying sites in the valleys include the important religious centre at Arminghall. Here, a temple, similar in style to Stonehenge but with timber uprights instead of stone, is associated with a number of burial mounds. No settlement sites of the Bronze Age (2000 – 800 B.C.) have been found in the area, but there is considerable evidence for the presence of these people here. Two burial mounds or round barrows remain on Eaton golf course out of a group of four, and bronze tools and weapons have been found scattered over the area. Late Bronze Age hoards of bronze tools and weapons have been found at Costessey, Hellesdon Hall, Unthank Road, Norgate Road and Eaton, indicating the sites of temporary smithies. During the Iron Age (about 800 B.C. – A.D. 43) the chief centre of activity was in the Yare valley, where pottery has been found in Markshall, Arminghall and Trowse parishes. There is reason to suppose that this was an important settlement area; this was perhaps a contributing factor in the siting of the Roman town *Venta Icenorum* at Caistor St. Edmunds. This town was the major settlement in the district during the Roman period (A.D. 43 – 410), but Roman roads probably crossed the site of the later city of Norwich. There is strong evidence for an east-west road from a river port at Brundall entering the city near Pilling Park, Harvey Lane, which continues through the grounds of Mousehold House and the reservoirs, and down Gas Hill to a river-crossing on the site of Bishop Bridge. It is uncertain if this crossing was by a bridge or through a ford. The line is continued along Bishopgate Street (where in the Middle Ages it was known as *Holmstrete*), St. Benedicts Street and Dereham Road almost to the present city boundary, where it changes direction slightly to run through Bowthorpe. There is a scatter of finds dating from the 1st to the 4th centuries A.D. related to this line, which for convenience may be called Holmstrete – Westwick Way. A north to south Roman road along

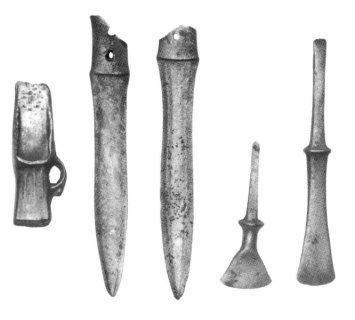

3 *Bronze tools and weapons from the Eaton hoard, one of several hoards from the Norwich area hidden by travelling smiths about 800 BC (Late Bronze Age).*

5 *4th century colour-coated ware pot from the site of the roman cemetery at the West Norwich hospital, beside the Holmestrete – Westwick Way roman road.*

The Origins of Norwich

either Ber Street or King Street has been suggested in the past, but there is no archaeological evidence for such a route. A few other finds have been made in central Norwich, but nothing to suggest more than the possibility of a farmstead. Other settlements have been found in the Yare valley at Eaton, and in the Wensum valley at Lakenham and Earlham, probably the homesteads of peasant farmers. The later prominence of Norwich as a port is foreshadowed by what is thought to be a quay on the river Yare at its confluence with the river Wensum; this continued in use from about A.D. 50 to 150.

Norwich grew out of a number of small settlements established on the gravel terraces. The archaeological evidence for this is scanty, but it is significant when considered in relation to certain place-names. Saxon material dating from the 6th century onwards has been found near St. Benedict's Gate, the western extremity of an area known as Westwick. The name occurs as *Westwic* in 12th century documents and the form of the name suggests that it originated before 850, as did the name *Coslania*. Coslany is an area on the north side of the river Wensum which is, on topographical grounds, a possible site for the 5th and 6th century settlement whose dead were buried on the higher ground now occupied by Eade Road. Middle Saxon occupation dating from the 8th – 9th centuries has been

2 *(left) The Yare valley from Whitlingham about 300,000 BC (Old Stone Age), showing typical animals and a man making a flint hand-axe.*

4 *Roman gold signet ring showing Cupid riding a sea-horse, found at Caistor-by-Norwich roman town.*

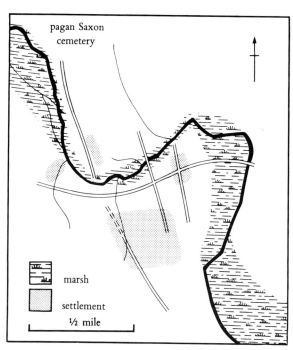

Map 1 *8th/9th century settlements with the east-west roman road and later roads.*

9

discovered in the Close, adjacent to the Holmstrete – Westwick Way Roman road. This settlement, perhaps called *Northwic,* lies on the eastern edge of the gravel terrace close to Bishop Bridge, the suggested river-crossing for the road. The importance of both this crossing and the nearby one at Fyebridge in Roman and Medieval times strongly suggests that one of these was the King's Ford, a name retained for the area known as Conesford. The 12th century spelling of this name *(Cunegesford)* shows that it is Danish in form and cannot therefore have originated before 900, but it almost certainly represents a Danish modification of an earlier Saxon name. The name Conesford is restricted today to an area at the south end of King Street, but there is nowhere in this area suitable for a ford. Perhaps the largest of the Middle Saxon settlements which eventually formed Norwich was Needham. This was probably centred beneath the later Norman Castle. None of these settlements were likely to be more than one or two farmsteads. By the mid 9th century there was almost certainly a local market in the area for the sale of surplus produce. It may have been in Needham, but it is unlikely that its site will ever be identified.

6 *6th century bronze brooch from the Anglo-Saxon cemetery at Eade Road.*

Late Saxon Norwich 850-1066

The name *Northwic* first appears for certain on coins of Aethelstan I of England, minted between 920 and 940. A single penny of the St. Edmund memorial issue produced in Danish East Anglia about A.D. 900 *may* bear the name of Norwich, but not all numismatists accept this. The form of the name suggests an origin for *Northwic* before 850, and it was probably the name of the settlement in the Close. The establishment of a fortified administrative and market centre here may have taken place during the forty years of Danish control of East Anglia from 879. It may have been deliberately created about 920 by Edward the Elder, King of Wessex, after he regained English control of East Anglia. Unfortunately archaeological evidence cannot be sufficiently closely dated to settle this problem. South of the river there is strong topographical evidence for a bank and ditch which enclosed much of the later Close and Tombland. Parts of the boundary can be traced in anomalies in the street plan (for details see Carter 1978, pp. 192-3). The northern section of this ditch may have run along the south side of the churchyard of St. Martin at Palace Plain towards Elm Hill, then along Elm Hill and Redwell Street. Bank Street and part of St. Faith's Lane may mark the southern edge while the eastern section was probably dug near to the junction of the gravel terrace and the marsh. This marsh was not part of *Northwic.*

A settlement north of the river was also defended and possibly was created as a trading settlement or suburb to the main fortified area to the south. A ditch, in places confirmed by excavation, has been traced along Whitefriars and Cowgate, and across Magdalen Street. The western ditch was found running south to Colegate between St. Georges Street and Calvert Street. It is uncertain if all these are contemporary. There is some evidence for remodelling

7 *Silver penny of Aethelstan of England (924 – 939). This is the earliest certain written record of the name Norwich (NORWIC).*

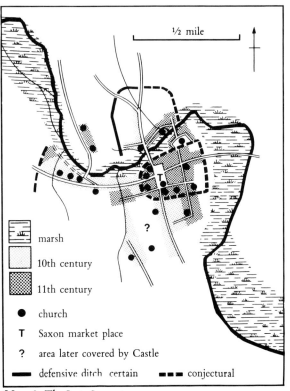

Map 2 *The Late Saxon town*

½ mile

marsh

10th century

11th century

● church

T Saxon market place

? area later covered by Castle

— defensive ditch certain ▪▪▪ conjectural

8 *Tombland looking south, the Erpingham gate on the left. This was the site of the Saxon market and of medieval and later fairs.*

9, 10 *10th century disc brooch and strap-end from a 10th/11th century timber church (brooch) and grave-yard (strap-end), excavated adjacent to Anglia Television. The dedication of the church is unknown.*

of the defences north of the river, perhaps after the attack in 1004 by Sweyn and his Vikings.

It is the southern fortified area which incorporated the Saxon settlement of *Northwic* and became the centre of the new town. Mints could only be established in *burhs,* the essential features of which were fortifications and a market. It was probably for geographical reasons that *Northwic* was selected as the *burh* rather than Needham. *Northwic* controlled three important river crossings, at Bishop Bridge, Whitefriars Bridge and Fyebridge; the two last were also protected on the north of the river by the defences there. There is a growing amount of archaeological evidence for the berthing of merchant ships on the south side of the river, near St. Martin's church. The ships were run onto the shelving sandy banks of the river on brushwood and unloaded onto the gravel terrace there known as *Bychel.* The goods would have been sold, together with local produce, in the market on Tombland.

There is no documentary evidence as to what was sold in this market. There is archaeological evidence for the import of such imperishable goods as pottery from the east Midlands, and millstones, swords and pottery, including wine vessels, from the Rhineland. It is probable too that such luxury articles as furs from Scandinavia and Russia, walrus ivory from Scandinavia and fine quality woollen cloths from Flanders, recorded for other parts of England, were unloaded at the Norwich water-front for sale in the market here. Farm produce from the Norwich area must have been very important, while other local products included locally-made pottery and iron tools; there is archaeological evidence for both iron-working and pottery-making. This latter industry probably began in the late 10th century to the west of the fortified settlement. It eventually stretched along Bedford Street and Pottergate (the street of potters) from St. Andrews Hill to Lower Goat Lane. Local smiths north of the river Wensum smelted iron ores from the local gravels to make weapons, knives and agricultural implements. There is archaeological evidence too, from wet sites, for the production of wooden, bone and leather objects, including shoes. Nevertheless farming was probably the major occupation

11

of most of the inhabitants of Norwich. Most of the pasture and arable plots were within the boundary of the borough. At least two water-mills were in use for grinding the grain; these were probably on the river Wensum in the Westwick area. There is some evidence for the importance of herrings in the economy of late 11th century Norwich, but it is not possible to be certain whether they were caught by fishermen from Norwich or from the new town of Yarmouth.

Because of the lack of documents, it is impossible to give any coherent picture of Late Saxon Norwich until the eve of the Norman Conquest. The information compiled in 1086 at the Domesday survey compares the situation in about 1065 with that after 20 years of Norman rule. The information is, however, frequently difficult to interpret.

By 1065 Norwich was administered separately from the rest of Norfolk. The inhabitants of the borough did not form a self-governing unit, but were responsible to a royal offical who collected the rents and taxes. The King received £20 a year and the Earl of East Anglia £10. The wealth of the borough is reflected by the proportion of tax-paying burgesses, 1,320 out of a total population of about 5,500. The community was divided into three lordships for judicial purposes. 1,238 of the burgesses were directly responsible to King Edward the Confessor, and to the Earl, then Gyrth Godwinsson, brother of Harold II. Harold had been a former Earl of East Anglia and still retained land here in his own right, with jurisdiction over 32 burgesses. The remaining 50 burgesses owed allegiance to Stigand, the Archbishop of Canterbury who had formerly held the See of East Anglia. About 40 churches and chapels are mentioned in the Domesday Survey, a further illustration of the wealth of the borough. The richest church was St. Michael on Tombland, close to the Earl's Palace.

The territorial limits of the borough at this date are not easy to define, but later documentary evidence shows that it was smaller than the area included within the circuit of the Medieval walls. It is possible that some of the land later taken into Norwich on the west may have been the 80 acres of arable land and three acres of meadow which the burgesses owned in the adjacent Hundred of Humbleyard. A study of the distribution of pottery of the period from archaeological excavations and from building sites suggests that south of the river expansion of settlement outside the fortified area had begun before the end of the 10th century. By 1066 the settlement of *Westwic* was linked to *Northwic* by 'ribbon development' along St. Benedicts Street.

The Normans and After 1066-1194

In 1066 the development of Norwich was interrupted and its course drastically changed by the Norman invasion of England. After the Conquest a Norman zone was created across the town. The three most important elements were the Castle, the Cathedral and the market place (the present provision market). This provided a new focus round which the Anglo-Norman borough developed, for, by the

end of the period the settlement had recovered from the shock of the Conquest and had acquired a new importance as a cathedral town and as a military and administrative centre.

The account in the Domesday Book of the borough in 1086 gives vivid, if confused, glimpses of the shattering effects of the Conquest and, probably even more, the revolt of the Earl in 1075. The number of English burgesses had fallen from 1,320 in 1066 to 665 in 1086. Thirty-two had fled – 22 of them to Beccles – while others may have lost their privileged status because they could no longer pay their dues. There were 480 cottagers who were too poor to pay anything, 50 houses from which the King received no rent and 297 houses which had been destroyed or were standing empty. The inhabitants had suffered from the exactions of Waleran, who seems to have farmed both Norwich and Colchester at some time in William's reign (that is he paid the King a lump sum and made what profit he could by collecting royal dues). There had also been disastrous fires. Land once held by the English was now in Norman hands; the burgesses had lost, among other things, 12½ acres of meadow and their church of Holy Trinity. The English population had declined, but taxes had gone up from £31 1s. 4d. in 1066 to £96 in 1086.

Nevertheless for many life must have continued much as it did before the Conquest. Many of the craftsmen continued to work in traditional ways and styles. This can be seen in the pottery which was made in Norwich in the Pottergate area until some time in the 12th century, and in some of the architecture of the churches.

Probably soon after the Conquest, William had a castle built here; it seems to have been his policy to have a royal castle in every county town. King Harold's brother Gyrth Godwinsson had been Earl of East Anglia and owned an official residence in Norwich. The building of a Norman castle underlined the fact that the power of the Godwins had been broken and made it possible for quite a small force of trained soldiers to intimidate and control the local population. Here, as everywhere in England, the vanquished outnumbered the victors. The first Norwich Castle was not a stone fortress, which would have taken too long to construct, but an earth and timber erection. The existing houses on the site (nearly 100) were demolished or commandeered and their occupants evicted; the townsfolk were forced to work on the defences. They must have hated the castle as a symbol of foreign domination, yet it provided protection, employment, and custom for the local craftsmen and for the traders in the market place just outside the fortifications.

This market place is assumed to be part of that 'French Borough' which Domesday Book tells us was created by Earl Ralf who, shortly after the Conquest, had been made Earl of East Anglia. He held this borough from the King in the same way as he held his country estates. Domesday Book records 41 French burgesses in the new settlement in 1086, plus 83 other inhabitants, some of whom may also have been burgesses. Domesday Book does not tell us where this French Borough was; it is believed it was in the Mancroft area which had been town fields before the Conquest. The church which Earl Ralf built was almost certainly the predecessor of St. Peter Mancroft. When Ralf rebelled in 1075 this borough, with all his other possessions, was seized by the King and, as far as we know, re-

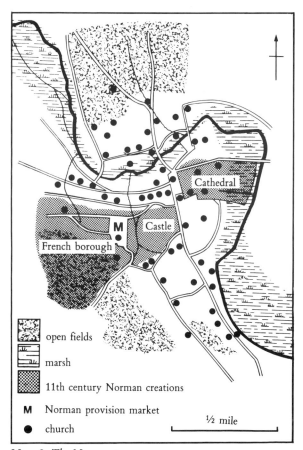

open fields

marsh

11th century Norman creations

M Norman provision market

● church

½ mile

Map 3 *The Norman town*

11 *12th century stone capital from Norwich cathedral, almost certainly part of the Norman cloisters and re-used in the 14th century.*

mained in royal hands ever afterwards. It is described in Domesday Book as if it were still a separate entity, but it seems likely that the two communities had merged by 1150 at the latest.

In 1094 the seat of the bishopric was established at Norwich and, two years later, Bishop Herbert de Losinga began to build a cathedral here; the completed portion was consecrated in 1101. On the northern side of the Cathedral was a palace for the Bishop (nearly finished when Losinga died in 1119) and on the south side a monastery to house up to 60 Benedictine monks and their staff. Part of the precinct lay in the manor of Thorpe but most of the new buildings were put up in the old *burh*. It is possible that many buildings there were destroyed during or after the 1075 revolt thus creating a large space. The Saxon market place of Tombland came under the control of the Priory and the church of St. Michael and the Earl's Palace were also swept away to enlarge the open space outside the Cathedral gates. This ruthless destruction of property and the establishment of a privileged community of foreign monks in their midst were hateful to the English inhabitants. There were in the future many bitter conflicts between the burgesses and the Priory, and even the Benedictine nunnery which was established at Carrow in 1146 was a source of irritation to the townsfolk. The Prioress' claim to take toll of corn sold in Norwich at the time of Carrow Fair was not settled until 1290, while disputes over common rights went on until 1521.

But though the conquerors and their innovations were disliked in Norwich, there is no doubt that they brought prosperity to the borough. The Normans were great builders; the erection of the Castle, the Cathedral, and houses like the Jew's house in King Street (now Wensum Lodge) must have provided work for scores of local people. Some of the skilled craftsmen and overseers may have been brought from abroad but Anglo-Saxon features, such as the round windows in the cloister wall at the Cathedral, show that English craftsmen shared in the work.

Pottery, lava millstones and schist hones show that overseas trade with the Rhineland and Scandinavia continued, while French pottery and Caen stone, which was imported by the shipload for buildings including the Castle and Cathedral, provide evidence for the opening up of trade with Normandy. Trade with other parts of England also continued.

In 1066 Norwich was one of the largest towns in England, with an Anglo-Danish population of about 5,500. By 1086, as a result of the Norman Conquest, only about 5,000 people were living here and a considerable number of them were aliens – Normans, Frenchmen, Bretons and Flemings. The Castle was garrisoned by foreigners, and most of the residents of the French Borough came from overseas. The monks who subsequently came to staff Norwich Cathedral Priory were Normans and, by 1144, there was a settled community of Jews who probably came from northern France and the Rhineland. Most of them lived in the present White Lion Street and the Haymarket area, but this Jewry was not a ghetto in which all Jews were obliged to live. An early synagogue probably stood close to the present Dove Street, and the remains of a flint house, perhaps built by Jurnet the Jew in about 1175, now form part of Wensum Lodge in King Street. Jurnet's son Isaac was one of the richest Jews in England. The Jews lived by money-lending (Christians were not allowed to do this; Jews were allowed to do little else). Consequently anyone who needed to borrow capital on a large scale had to apply to the Jews. It is known that they lent money to the Abbey at Bury St. Edmunds and it is more than likely that the building of Norwich Cathedral was financed in the same way. The

12 *North face of Norwich Castle keep, built in the 12th century, showing the original facing of flint on lower half and stone above.*

13 *Contemporary caricatures of Norwich Jews – Isaac son of Jurnet, Mosse Mokke and his wife – on a document dated 1232/33.*

Jews were protected by royal officials because they were legally the King's chattels. In 1144 the Norwich Jews, accused of the ritual murder of the boy later known as St. William, were taken into the Castle by the Sheriff to protect them from the fury of the people.

In 1194 the population of Norwich was mixed. It was also divided, for the built-up area was not a single administrative unit; the burgesses had no control over the Castle 'Fee' or the Cathedral Precinct. These two 'liberties' were cut out of the old Anglo-Saxon borough and this permanently altered the pattern of settlement.

The Self-Governing City
1194-1348

In this period Norwich grew in size and wealth. It was the sixth richest town in England in 1334, with an estimated population of about 6,000. The remains of many large merchant houses – for example the undercroft of Strangers' Hall, about 1320 – show the wealth of the trading classes.

This prosperity was due to the City's position as the chief market town of one of the most thickly populated districts of Medieval England. The main market place became so crowded that subsidiary markets developed. Horses, for example, were sold outside the churchyard of St. Stephen's, in what is now Rampant Horse Street. Into all these markets came wool for the weavers and food for the citizens – bread corn, barley for brewing, pigs, sheep and cattle, fish from sea and river, shell-fish, poultry and dairy produce, vegetables and herbs, and salt (the essential Medieval preservative) from saltpans on the coast and marshes. In return, the peasants could buy the products of the City. Over 130 trades and occupations are recorded in 13th century Norwich, some very specialised and needing a larger market then even a big city could supply. Leather-working was perhaps the most important industry. Hides from the slaughter houses and goat-skins from the market formed the basis of this industry; the skins were prepared by one group of craftsmen – tanners, tawyers and curriers, while others made them into jerkins, gloves, belts, harness, parchment and many other useful things. There were also textile workers producing woollen and worsted cloth, and metalworkers, whose products ranged from large and costly objects like church bells, to needles, knives and miscellaneous ironmongery. The Prior, the Bishop and the richer merchants gave employment to stone carvers, glass painters, illuminators, goldsmiths and other highly skilled persons. The needs of the ordinary citizens were met by the building craftsmen who put up their houses, and the makers of wooden bowls, spoons, tallow candles and so on who provided the meagre furnishing.

But though most of the commodities sold in Norwich were of local origin there were also imported goods. Foreign merchants frequented the City (a wine merchant from Cologne is mentioned as early as 1144), though only the woad merchants from Amiens and Corbeil were allowed to live here. Some of the imports were necessities. Medieval people ate more fish than meat and salted herring from the Scania district of Sweden supplemented home supplies. Many materials essential for Norwich industries came from abroad. Building craftsmen used Caen stone and imported, as well as home-grown, timber. Pitch and tar, like the timber, came from the great forests of northern Europe. For the metalworkers there was steel from Sweden, France and Spain. The textile workers were fortunate in that the wool they used was home-grown, but even they needed olive oil from Spain, and dye-stuffs from France, Asia Minor and the Far East, wood-ash from northern Europe and alum from Asia Minor as mordants to fix their dyes. Millstones were imported from the Rhineland, while leather workers were called cordwainers after the fine skins from Cordova in Spain which they used for their best work.

14 *13th century stone mould for a plaque depicting the Massacre of the Innocents, found near London Street.*

The other imports were luxuries. Only the rich could afford wine from Gascony, Oriental spices, choice furs from Scandinavia, fine woollen cloth from Flanders and silk cloth from Italy and the East, and decorative pottery from the Low Countries and France. The best beeswax for candles was imported, as was the best table salt and a little, very expensive, sugar from the Mediterranean. Successful Norwich merchants could afford to buy such things from their profits from local sales and from exports to the Continent of wool, fleeces, hides, dairy produce and corn.

The wealth of Norwich and the employment it offered brought a stream of immigrants from the countryside, both free peasants and serfs seeking freedom (after they had been three days in the City they could not be recovered by their lords without a trial; after a year and a day they could not be recovered at all). These immigrants were English; their coming helped to reduce the proportion of aliens in the population, as did the decline of the Jewish community, which suffered greatly from royal exploitation and popular persecution. When they were finally expelled, with all other English Jews, in 1290, there were only 17 impoverished households left.

Norwich was now rich enough to buy privileges and after the death of Henry II in 1189 the Kings of England were much more willing to allow boroughs to become self-governing. So in 1194 Norwich obtained a charter from Richard I which gave the citizens the right to elect their own Reeve to govern the City, which had hitherto been controlled by a royal official. A lump sum was to be paid to the King every year in place of the rents, tolls and other dues which up to then had been collected by Crown agents. In 1256 the City obtained the right to have cases which had previously been heard in the royal courts at Westminster or elsewhere, tried in Norwich. The effect of all this was to exclude royal officials, including the Sheriff of the County, from the City's affairs. Norwich was still a

royal borough but the citizens' own elected representatives now governed in the King's name.

In this period the defences of the City were strengthened and the enclosed area greatly extended. There is documentary evidence of the construction of a ditch in 1150 in the Westwick area, but we do not know whether this was an isolated work or part of a general reorganisation of the town defences. We know more about the new bank and ditch which were being made in 1253. To the north of the City the defences were advanced into Taverham Hundred to the line of Bakers Road and Magpie Road and thence to the river Wensum, cutting through the Prior's manor of Pockthorpe. On the south, the defences of Westwick, Conesford and the French Borough were joined along the line of the present Barn Road, Grapes Hill, Chapelfield Road and Queens Road. The area thus enclosed by bank, ditch and river – nearly a square mile – was enormous compared with that of most Medieval boroughs. In 1297 the City obtained permission from the King to compel all inhabitants to contribute to the cost of constructing a masonry wall on top of the bank. This was a colossal task; the completed wall with its gates and towers contained about 37,000 tons of masonry, enought to build 80 small churches. The work was not completed until 1334.

Inside the walled City there were, by 1348, large areas of ecclesiastical land whose position has in some cases determined the pattern of settlement to the present day. In 1194 the most important was the precinct of the Cathedral Priory. By 1248 there was also the extensive site of the Chapel-in-the-Fields, originally a hospital, but soon housing a resident community or 'college' of priests. In 1249 Bishop Walter de Suffield founded the Great Hospital in Bishopgate Street for poor chaplains (that is, priests who had no church living) when they were too old or too ill to work any longer. The parish church of St. Helen on the

15 *Bishop Bridge with medieval gate built 1342/43 by Richard Spynk: one of the 12 gates of Norwich's medieval defences. Gateway removed 1791.*

16 *Ethelbert Gate, leading into the Cathedral precinct, built by the citizens following the 1272 riot.*

16

other side of the road was demolished and the hospital chapel took its place. The meadow lying between the new building and the river was given to the Hospital by William de Dunwich. Before 1348 the Friars had established four large precincts. At first they had occupied little land; they hired small houses in poor quarters of the City, in which they lived very simply without servants, using parish churches for their services. But as their numbers and revenues increased, they enlarged their convents and built large churches with 'preaching naves' open to the public, so that their original sites became too restricted. Sometimes they moved, as the Dominicans did in 1307, from their original position in Black Boys Street, north of Colegate. Others enlarged the original site, absorbing houses, roads and even parish churches – as when the Franciscans, about 1300, acquired St. John in Southgate, near Rose Lane. The precincts of the Dominicans between St. Andrews Street and the river, of the Francisans and the Augustinians in King Street, and of the Carmelites in Cowgate, formed large enclosed areas, sometimes blocking or diverting ancient rights of way, within whose walls no secular building could take place.

The citizens wanted to make Norwich a self-contained, self-governing entity and succeeded in gaining control of most of the Castle Fee in 1345. But they had no authority inside the ecclesiastical precincts and consequently a great deal of the eastern part of the City, though inside their boundary, was outside their jurisdiction. This caused friction between the City and the Cathedral Priory. The monks accused the citizens of enclosing and trespassing on their lands when digging the town ditch in 1253. The citizens would not admit the monks' claim to control certain areas outside their precinct walls, such as Bishopgate Street and Tombland, and there were bitter disputes about common rights at Eaton and Lakenham which dragged on for many years. A quarrel, which began as a brawl between some citizens and some of the Priory servants at the Trinity Fair in June 1272, culminated in a full scale attack on the Priory on 9th August, during which the precinct gate, the church of St. Ethelbert inside it, the bell tower and most of the wooden buildings of monastery, were destroyed. The citizens were severely punished for this; later they re-built the Ethelbert Gate as an act of reparation, the chapel above the Gate being a substitute for the ruined church. In the final settlement the monks were given control of Bishop Bridge and elaborate arrangements were made to divide the Tombland fair-ground equitably between monks and citizens.

This was perhaps the greatest setback that the City experienced in this period, but it was not the only one. In 1215 the barons who had rebelled against King John invited the French Prince Louis to seize the throne of England. He invaded England in May 1216, and, even after the death of John in October, made determined efforts to take the Kingdom from the new King, Henry III, then a child of nine. Louis seized Norwich Castle early in 1217 and his troops plundered the City. In 1266 another group of rebel barons – 'The Disinherited' – raided Norwich, sacked it, and carried off many of the rich citizens to their strongholds in the Isle of Ely, holding them to ransom. In 1307 the citizens complained that John de Lovetot had seized cattle worth £300 in Norwich and district, and had driven them into the Castle.

Such disasters, together with the high death rate, explain why even a rich city like Norwich grew so slowly; it also makes it clear that, although the Castle protected the City while the central government was strong, it could be a liability in times of civil war.

The Black Death and After 1348-1485

In January 1349, the Black Death appeared in Norwich. This was bubonic plague (carried by black rats) accompanied by contagious pneumonic plague. The epidemic lasted throughout 1349 and there were further outbreaks in 1361-2 and 1369. We have no means of knowing how many people in Norwich died in 1349 (Blomefield's figure of over 57,000 is absurd) but the City may well have lost two-fifths of a population of about 6,000 and at least half its clergy. Four parish churches ceased to function because there were neither parishioners nor priests to keep them going. It was because of the desperate shortage of educated clergy after the Black Death that William Bateman (Bishop of Norwich, 1344 – 1355) founded Trinity Hall in Cambridge to train more priests. A Roll of 1357 lists shops and market stalls left empty for so long that they had fallen into ruin, and, after the plague and famine of 1369, the overcrowded churchyard of St. Peter Mancroft was extended southwards by taking in part of what had been the cloth market.

By the end of the century, however, the City had recovered from the Black Death and was indeed very prosperous. There were about 6,000 people living in Norwich in 1377. Many of them were peasants from marginal lands no longer worth cultivating; Norwich could offer them work, especially in the textile industry which was now rapidly expanding.

The manufacture of worsted cloth, which is said to take its name from a Norfolk village, presumably began in the countryside. But by 1300 worsted as well as woollen cloth was being made in Norwich and by the reign of Richard II (1377 – 1399) Norwich was the chief seat of worsted manufacture. In other cloth-making districts, workers were leaving the towns and settling near the fast flowing streams which turned the fulling mills. This did not happen in Norfolk because worsted cloth was not fulled and Norwich remained the industrial centre. By the Statutes of 1444 and 1467 the Wardens of the Norwich Worsted Weavers' Craft Guild were empowered to regulate the industry throughout East Anglia.

Wool dealers, centred on Mattishall, collected the Norfolk wool and sold it in small quantities to the spinners, who combed it, spun it with a distaff and spindle, and twisted it in a twistering mill. The yarn was then usually taken to market and sold direct to the weavers. The cloth was finished by the calenderers, who pressed it, and the shearmen who did the final tidying up. Some cloth was dyed, but most of it was sold 'white'.

Most of the Norwich weavers were small working craftsmen; the people who made the money were the wool dealers, who were countrymen, and the merchants, in-

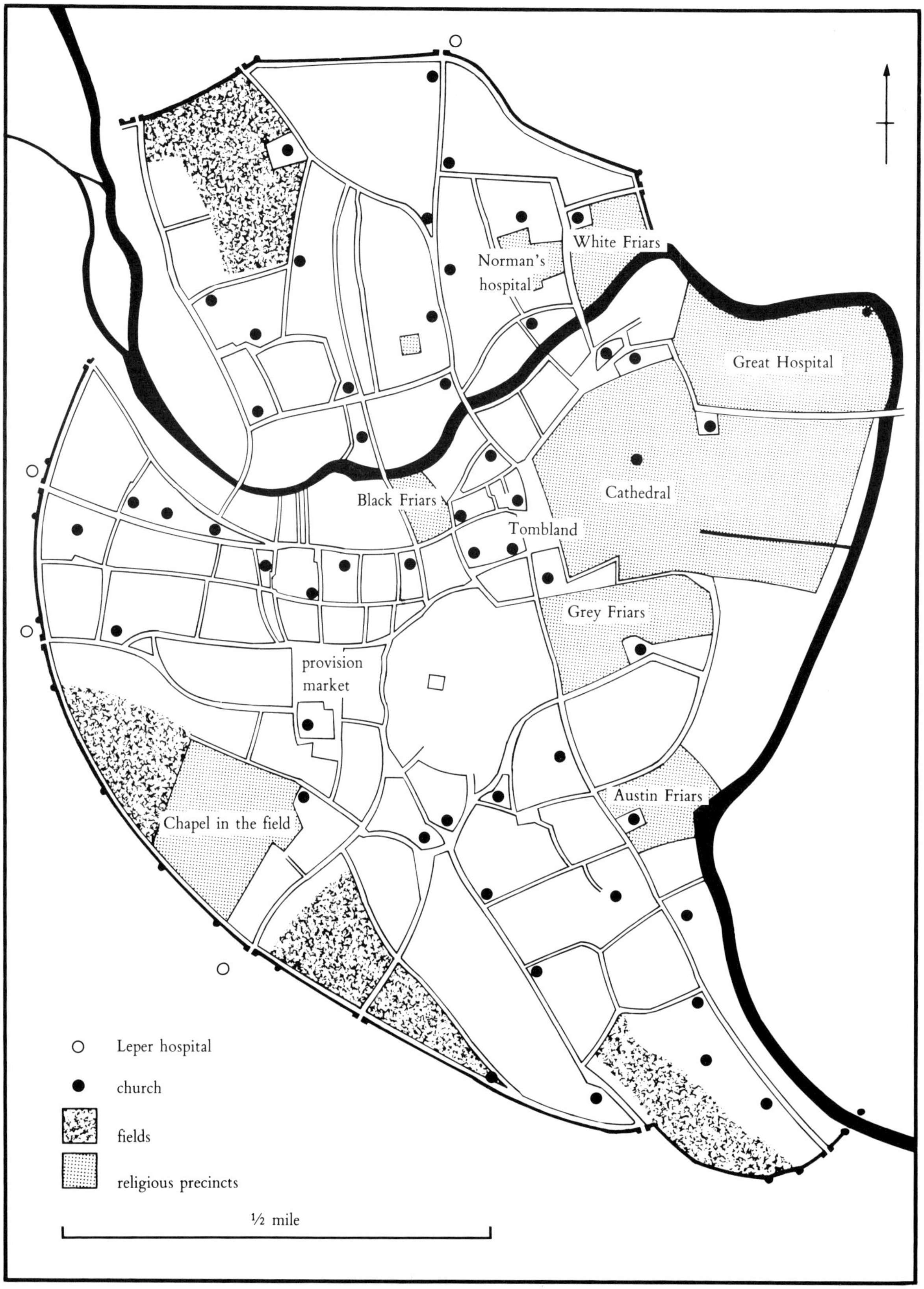
White Friars
Norman's hospital
Great Hospital
Cathedral
Black Friars
Tombland
Grey Friars
provision market
Austin Friars
Chapel in the field
Leper hospital
church
fields
religious precincts
½ mile

Map 4 *The walled city, about 1348*

cluding the members of the small Norwich group of Merchant Adventurers, who sold cloth in the Netherlands. In 1522, William Hart (Mayor in 1512 and 1519) was chosen as one of the provincial representatives at the meetings of the London Merchant Adventurers.

At the end of the 14th century a great deal of worsted cloth was exported from Yarmouth or from London to commercial centres in the Netherlands and Italy, whence it was distributed to northern Europe and the Mediterranean countries. This was part of a general expansion of English export trade in the reign of Richard II. Much worsted cloth was also sold in England, where it was used for hangings, curtains, fine clothes for laymen and summer habits for monks.

There were also many weavers of 'dornix', a type of cloth much used for bed curtains, coverlets, wall hangings and the 'carpets' which covered chests and tables. It is not clear how this cloth differed from worsted, although some kinds of 'dornix' had some linen thread in them.

As in other boroughs, power came to be concentrated in the hands of a small group of rich merchants (almost all the 15th century Mayors were merchants of one kind or another). These men often married the daughters of county gentry, and themselves owned country estates, like William Appleyard (first Mayor of Norwich in 1404) who married one of the Cleres of Ormesby, and was Lord of the Manors of Bracon Ash and Intwood. They controlled the whole economic life of the community and were therefore naturally blamed when business flagged, especially as they seemed to get richer and richer, while others became poorer.

In 1380 the would-be oligarchs obtained a charter giving the bailiffs and the Twenty-Four (a committee of leading citizens) power to make and alter by-laws. The other citizens later complained that this had been done without their knowledge or consent. When, by the Charter of 1404, the bailiffs were replaced by a Mayor and two Sheriffs, there were bitter disputes as to whether these should be chosen by the governing clique of the Twenty-Four or by the freemen. A compromise was reached in 1414, but the real power remained in the hands of the Mayor and Sheriffs, and the 24 aldermen who, once elected, sat for life. The Charters of 1414 and 1417 also made Norwich, like other big and successful boroughs, a legal corporation and a county in itself. But the attempts of the City to exert authority outside its walls met with a series of humiliating rebuffs until the limits of the County of Norwich were clearly defined in the Charter of 1556.

Trading inside the city had always been regulated by the civic authorities, who fixed the prices of bread and ale, punished people who gave short weight or sold faulty goods, and sought to discourage middlemen. But from 1377 onwards control was intensified. The ruling oligarchy bought up shops and market stalls and raised market tolls. In 1379 they bought the Common Staithes and ordered that all boats should unload there. In 1384 they obtained the block of property between Pottergate and the market place; the southern part became a Common Inn and the part adjacent to Pottergate a sale hall (the Worsted Seld). Country weavers wishing to sell their cloth in the City were obliged to trade here.

The civic authorities were also determined to control industry, but here the position was complicated by the ex-

17 *Thomas Elys (Sheriff 1452, Mayor 1460, 1465, 1474, died 1487) and his wife Margaret. One of the rich merchants who rebuilt St Peter Mancroft church.*

istence of craft guilds. In every industry there were three classes of worker: the apprentices who were learning the craft, the journeymen who were trained craftsmen employed by the day, and the masters who were the employers, though many also worked with their own hands. Each craft had its own guild to which all the masters had to belong but from which the apprentices and journeymen were excluded. The elected Wardens and Searchers (or inspectors) of each craft issued and enforced detailed instructions about technique and standards of production; they also fixed prices. They controlled the apprenticeship of boys to the craft and the eventual acceptance of some of them as master craftsmen and guild members. Some of the money which a guild derived from the fees paid by its members was spent on pensions for guildsmen who had become too old or too ill to work. All craft guilds took a corporate part in the religious life of the time and later, in the early 16th century, there was an elaborate procession of all the guilds on Corpus Christi day. But in this period most of the money devoted to religious purposes was spent on providing handsome funerals for deceased guildsmen and on paying for Masses to be said for their souls. In the 12th and 13th centuries the City's rulers distrusted the craft guilds and tried, but failed, to suppress them. By the 15th century the official attitude had changed; craft guilds were recognised not merely as legitimate trade associations, but as an integral part of the City's government. In

18 *The undercroft of the old Tollhouse, all that remains of the predecessor of the early 15th century Guildhall. It was used as a prison.*

19 *Dragon in a mid 15th century roof spandrel of Robert Toppys' hall, the Old Barge, King Street. The hall was used for the display of goods for sale.*

1415 it was enacted that all the freemen (who were the privileged section of the inhabitants) must be craft guild members. Henceforth the civic authorities controlled industry through the guilds, whose officials, when elected, were formally presented to the Mayor for his approval; the City took half the fines they imposed for bad work.

All these measures meant not only more control, but also more profit for the ruling clique, and they were soon able to embark on an ambitious building programme. Between 1399 and 1430 the City re-built the Cow Tower, the Market Cross, the Guildhall and the City water mills (the New Mills).

At the end of the 14th century Norwich was thriving but not peaceful. The poorer people resented the tyranny of the rich and many of them sympathised with the rebellious serfs who occupied the City during the Peasants' Revolt in June 1381. In the 15th century the inhabitants were even more restless and discontented, while the City as a whole was much less prosperous. During the Wars of the Roses Norwich was inevitably affected by the anarchy in the countryside which is so vividly described in the Paston Letters. Worsted exports declined, for cloth made in the Netherlands from a mixture of Norfolk and Spanish wool was capturing the Continental markets. The new fairs established in 1482 were a failure, and by 1486 there were no stall-holders. Some of the great merchants continued to amass wealth and spend some of it on fine buildings like the present church of St. Peter Mancroft, which was re-built and reconsecrated in 1455. As the gap widened between the rich few and the impoverished many, the oligarchy became more powerful and also, of course, more unpopular.

Early Tudor Norwich 1485-1556

Norwich paid £1,704 in taxes in 1523-7, more than any other provincial town in England, but most of this large sum was contributed by the comparatively small number of very rich men who dominated this community of not more than 10,000 people. Many of these men had country estates, as well as businesses in the City and overseas. The career of John Marsham, who was Mayor in 1518, is typical. He came from the country and in due course inherited his father's property at Stratton Strawless. He was apprenticed in Norwich and later became a freeman of the City as a grocer, that is as a merchant dealing in imported foodstuffs. He married into a Suffolk county family and on the windows of the house which he built to the east of Strangers' Hall were displayed the coats of arms of himself and his wife. His son Thomas Marsham was Mayor in 1554; of his grandsons, Christopher Layer was Mayor twice and his brother Thomas three times. Men like these could afford to spend a great deal of money improving their houses, as Nicholas Sotherton (Mayor in 1539) did at Strangers' Hall, and adorning them with Flemish tapestries and magnificent gold and silver plate. They built for themselves elaborate tombs, like the terra-cotta tomb-chest of Robert Jannys (Mayor in 1517 and 1524) in St. George's church in Colegate. The Thorpe chapel at St. Michael Coslany church, about 1500, is the most impressive remaining example of the chantry chapels which they erected and endowed in order that prayers should be said for them after they had died.

They also spent lavishly on public buildings. In the first 35 years of the 16th century, for example, the City churches of St. Peter Permountergate, St. Andrew, St. George Colegate and St. Stephen, were wholly or partly re-built and an ornate Council Chamber was constructed in the Guildhall in 1535. Yet the majority of inhabitants were poor and growing poorer, and even their rich masters became alarmed at the decline of the town when, in 1544, they had to pay Andrew Robinson 7s. 10d. to clear the market place which was overgrown with weeds.

Almost all provincial boroughs complained of 'decay' in the early 16th century. Some of their complaints were no doubt exaggerated in the hope of tax relief, but Norwich had genuine problems. Worsted exports had dwindled almost to nothing, and other industries were stagnating.

In 1550 there were complaints that weavers and building craftsmen were leaving the City; the population was static, if not actually declining. In 1554 the Assembly took action against men who, having qualified as freemen, moved out into the county so that they no longer paid City rates, though they still sold their goods there toll free. The Government tried, but often in vain, to check this drift from the towns; in 1524, for example, they ordered that all worsted cloth, wherever woven, should be finished in Norwich.

In the City the conditions under which a craftsman did his work and the price he could get for it were controlled, not only by the guild and by the Corporation, as in former times, but now also by central Government. A Statute of 1504 laid down that all craft regulations must be approved by the Government, so in 1511 we find the Norwich worsted weavers submitting their revised rules for the Chancellor's approval. So much regulation meant complication, frustration and delay, especially as the aim of the guild, as well as the City and the Government, was to keep things as they always had been. Their answer to a slump was to maintain quality while reducing production, rather than seek new techniques or new markets. In 1511 for example, the Worsted Weavers' Guild laid down that all members must first have served as apprentices for seven years from the age of 14, and that no master weaver might have more than four apprentices, or more than five looms. But nothing the authorities could do prevented Norfolk wool (including that from the Cathedral Priory flocks) being smuggled out to rival cloth-makers in Flanders, or sold to country weavers in Suffolk or Essex. Nor could they stop craftsmen leaving the City to live in villages where they could practice several trades instead of being confined to one highly specialised occupation.

During this period the City must often have presented a dilapidated and even ruinous appearance. Several bad fires are recorded in the early 16th century, those of 1505 and 1507 being especially devastating. Blomefield said that 1,718 houses were burnt in four days in April 1507, mostly by the riverside, around Tombland and in St. Andrew's parish. Many of the burnt sites remained derelict until the City obtained powers in 1534 to compel owners to rebuild their houses, or at least to enclose their land with a wall.

Many buildings were demolished or reconstructed as a consequence of the secularisation of ecclesiastical property which accompanied the Reformation. Norwich lost 14 parish churches during the 16th century, mostly under the Act of 1535/6 which allowed two adjacent parishes to be united and one church dispensed with, provided that the churches were less than a mile apart and that one of them was worth no more than £6 a year. Some of these churches were pulled down altogether, others gutted and left in ruins. St. Mary the Less was leased by the Corporation, and used first as a sale-hall, and then as a church for the French-speaking refugees.

Between 1538 and 1548 all the monasteries, colleges of secular priests and chantries within the present boundaries of the City were dissolved. Of the large areas of church land whose position had so markedly affected the plan of the Medieval City, only the Cathedral Close and the Great Hospital site remained intact. The buildings of the Franciscan and Augustinian Friars in King Street and those of the Carmelites in Cowgate were demolished and their pre-

20 Robert Jannys (Sheriff 1509, Mayor 1517, 1524, died 1530) was a grocer and a great benefactor to the city.

21 Merchant's mark and arms of Robert Browne (Mayor 1522), who rebuilt the west end of St Stephens church, where the shield can be seen outside at top of N.W. corner of the nave.

22 Late 15th century religious medallion showing Virgin and Child from a house in Pottergate built about 1470 and burnt down in April 1507.

23 *18th century painting of Robert Kett and other rebels receiving the Earl of Warwick's Herald under the Oak of Reformation on Mousehold Heath.*

cincts, because of their position in the heart of the City, were soon built over. Some ecclesiastical buildings were pulled down and their materials sold, but others were turned to secular uses. The Corporation bought the chapel of the former Carnary College in the Close and used it to house the Grammar School. They also purchased the Dominican Friary as a general utility building; consequently the huge church, though secularised, was preserved. All the hospitals in Norwich were threatened by the Act abolishing chantries, but the Corporation managed to retain most of them and used them for poor-houses, or for the pest-houses in which plague victims were isolated. The Great Hospital became a home for old men and women, the chancel of its church being divided into wards, though part of the nave was still used for worship. One effect of the Dissolution on Norwich was, therefore, to make available many new building sites and a great deal of cheap building material, together with numbers of disused, but still serviceable edifices. The amount of ecclesiastical land was diminished and consequently the area over which the City could exercise effective authority was enlarged. The Close, though now acknowledged to be part of the City, was still exempt from civic control, but after 1550 this was the only remaining 'liberty'.

Further destruction resulted from Kett's rebellion in 1549. The rebel army, encamped on Mousehold Heath, controlled the City, where there were many people who sympathised with this revolt of the yeomen against the rich sheepfarming landlords who were annexing or monopolising the commons. Some of the townsfolk were killed in the fighting and their houses were burnt down. Some had to help feed Kett's men and the Government troops

who were quartered here. Civic possessions suffered – Bishop Bridge Gate was damaged and Whitefriars Bridge was demolished; buildings on the Common Staithe and at the Great Hospital were burnt and the fences of the Town Close common thrown down. After the rebels were defeated, the grim business of revenge and punishment began. Kett was hanged at Norwich Castle on 7th December; at least 48 other men were executed in the City, some of whom were Norwich men. The Chamberlain's list of market stalls in this year shows that several were vacant because the tenants had joined the rebels and had either been executed or had fled.

Though this period was one of disruption and decline, there was still some progress. Two new industries were introduced. Felt hat-making was established by 1543 when the Craft Guild was officially recognised. Formerly these hats had been imported from France and Flanders and the craft may well have been started in Norwich by French immigrants, for six of the 16 Frenchmen recorded in Norwich in 1542 were hatters. It is doubtful, however, if this industry did the City much lasting good; it was never large and when the authorities tried to raise standards their regulations were flouted, and the hatters eventually moved to the country beyond their control.

Russell weaving was less troublesome. In 1554 Thomas Marsham, who was a mercer, persuaded a few weavers from the Netherlands to settle in Norwich, and provided them with looms so that they could produce russells and sateens – textiles which were proving dangerous rivals to the traditional Norwich worsted in the overseas market. The russell weavers never produced more than a few hundred cloths a year, but they were important because they showed how traditional industry could be improved by using workers and techniques from abroad.

There was success also, after centuries of dispute, in the vexed question of the commons. Many of the inhabitants kept domestic animals and needed pasture for them. In 1205 the City had bought grazing rights on the Priory commons between St. Stephen's Gate and the villages of Eaton and Lakenham. In 1523 the City acquired a common about which they had quarrelled with Carrow Abbey for centuries; in the next year they bought from the Cathedral Priory 80 acres of the Eaton-Lakenham common, which was fenced in to become the Town Close or City common. They also obtained control of the fairs on Tombland and the Magdalen fair at Sprowston, both formerly the property of the Church.

The Strangers in Norwich 1556-1642

Perhaps it was the modest success of the Russell Weavers' Fellowship that persuaded the City authorities in 1565 to arrange for 30 households of religious refugees from the Netherlands to settle permanently in Norwich. Six of the households were French-speaking Walloons and the rest, known as the 'Dutch', spoke Dutch or Flemish. There were already 174 refugees in Norwich when these official immigrants arrived and more soon followed, so that by the beginning of 1579 there were about 6,000 aliens in a total population of just over 16,000. Most of these Strangers were cloth-workers, and the intention was that they should manufacture types of cloth new to Norwich and teach the local weavers how to make them. The Strangers certainly produced a great deal of cloth and recaptured the export market, but they were reluctant to teach their techniques and the Norwich weavers were slow to learn them, so that most of the 'new draperies' were produced by aliens until after 1600.

When they first came the refugees had powerful protectors, but most of the inhabitants disliked them as foreigners and feared them as business rivals. Yet when, in May and June 1570, John Throgmorton and other Norfolk gentry tried to "raise up the commons and levy the power and put the Strangers out of the City of Norwich" there was little response from the citizens. Only two of those punished for this rebellion were Norwich men. It was felt that the Strangers had come to stay, but that they could and should be controlled.

The authorities issued a mass of regulations designed to encourage the Strangers to produce new types of cloth and sell them wholesale to Norwich merchants, and to discourage them from doing anything else. 'The Orders for the Strangers in Norwich', dated 20th April 1571, laid down, among other things, that the Strangers were not to walk in the streets after curfew had rung, and they were not to buy skins without a permit. Shoemakers and cobblers were to have their windows screened by a lattice three feet high and were only to work for, or sell to, other aliens. Later, Strangers were forbidden to work as shoemakers, to bake white bread, and to sell aquavita in the

Certayne versis / writtene by Thomas Brooke Getleman / in the tyme of his imprysonment / the daye before his deathe / who suffered at Norwich / the 30. of August. 1570.

all   ing

I Languishe as I lye /
And death doth make me thrall /
To cares which death shall sone cut of /
And sett me quyt of all.

yett feble fleshe would faynt /
To feale so sharpe a fyght /
Saue Fayth in Christ / doth comfort me /
And fleithe such fancy quyght.

For fyndyng forth howe frayle /
Eache worldly state doth stande /
I hould him blyst / that fearyng God /
Is redd of such a band.

For he that longest lyues /
And Nestors yeares doth gayne /
Hath so much more accompte to make / *he hath*
And fyndyth Lyfe but vayne.

What cawse ys then to quayle /
I am called before /
To tast the Joyes which Christis bloode /
Hath bowght and layde in store.

No no / no greter Joye /
Can eny hart posses /
Then throwgh the death to gayne a lyfe /
Wyth hym in blyssednes.

Who sende the Quene long lyfe /
Much Joye and contries peace /
Her Cowncell health / hyr fryndes good lucke /
To all ther Joyes increase.

Thus puttyng vppe my greaues /
I grownde my lyfe on God /
And thanke hym with most humble hart /
And mekelye kysse his rodde.

Finis / q' Thomas Brooke.

Seane / and allowyd / accordynge to the Quenes Maiestyes Innunction.

God saue the Quene

Imprynted at Norwich in the Paryshe of Saynct Andrews / by Anthony de Solempne. 1570.

24 *Verses written just before his death by Thomas Brooke, a conspirator against the Strangers in 1570, and printed by a Stranger, Anthony de Solempne, Norwich's first printer.*

streets. It was not until 1598 that resident aliens could become freemen of the City on the same terms as natives.

Their religious views also caused trouble. John Parkhurst, Bishop of Norwich in 1565, was sympathetic and let the French-speaking community hold their services in his private chapel. But in the 17th century the Bishops were increasingly hostile, especially Matthew Wren, Bishop of Norwich from December 1635 to May 1638, who was determined that the foreign churches should eventually be closed and that all the Strangers should be made to worship in the parish churches, as soon as they spoke English well enough to follow the service. Many left

25 *Rev. William Bridge, Rector of St Peter Hungate, a Puritan refugee who lived in Rotterdam 1636 – 41, becoming minister of the English church there.*

27 *Bowl dated 1617 made in North Holland, found near Charing Cross. Much 17th century imported Dutch pottery has been found in Norwich.*

26 *One of four silver beakers made c.1580 by William Cobbold of Norwich for use in the Dutch church, now Blackfriars' Hall.*

because of this and returned to Holland, which was now independent and able to offer religious freedom not only to returning refugees but also to fugitive Norfolk Puritans. Nevertheless a small foreign community remained and services in French continued until 1832.

The attitude of Norwich people to the Strangers varied from cautious approval to unqualified hostility and consequently it was a long time before the foreigners were absorbed. They formed two distinct groups each with its own church, the Dutch in Blackfriars Hall, the French eventually in the church of St. Mary the Less. Each group had its own local government organisation, its own cloth hall in the old Dominican buildings and its own local defence force. There was no distinct foreign quarter, but most of the Strangers, as one would expect, lived in the industrial districts in the north of the City on either side of the river Wensum.

In the reign of Elizabeth I many more apprentices entered worsted weaving than any other trade, but comparatively few became freemen. Either they worked all their lives as ill-paid journeymen after they had finished their apprenticeship, or they were operating as master craftsmen without taking up their freedom as they were supposed to do. It was not the worsted weavers who made great fortunes and attained high civic office, but the cloth merchants (mercers), and the men who dealt in imported food stuffs (grocers), or in clothing (tailors).

Throughout the reign of Elizabeth I there were always about 125 grocers in the City. They included the City's richest and most influential men – nearly half the Elizabethan Mayors were grocers. Up to 1585 their supplies came from Antwerp. When, in that year, the great commercial city was sacked, things became more difficult both for the grocers and for the mercers, for Antwerp was also a cloth mart. The grocers must have had many customers outside the City itself; so must the dealers in clothes, for there were exceptionally large numbers of tailors in the City (about 170, at any given time). There were also many shoemakers and smaller groups of glovers and hatters. Elizabethan Norwich was thus a place where the local gentry, especially perhaps the lesser gentry who rarely or never went to London, could buy imported food stuffs, medicines, and their best clothes. Up to 1600 it was those engaged in this trade in luxuries who made the money, because it was not until after that date that the native Norwich weavers themselves began to make the new types of cloth which the Strangers had introduced. The heavy bays continued to be produced by the Dutch only, but the lightweight coloured cloths which the French-speaking Walloons produced were similar to the traditional worsted, and by the end of the period the 'new draperies' were being made by native weavers and sold as 'Norwich stuffs' in France, Spain, Portugal and Italy. The experiment of 1565 had proved a success, but it was not a quick or easy victory, if only because the needs of the changed and expanding industry conflicted with long established traditions embodied in craft rules, municipal regulations and Acts of Parliament.

In the early 17th century the Norwich weavers were searching anxiously for wool, yarn and labour. Norwich worsted had always been made from Norfolk wool, but this was unsuitable for the new stuffs. Wool had to be brought in from the Midlands and not until 1617 was an adequate supply assured. Similarly, the local spinners could not produce enough yarn to keep the weavers busy and additional supplies had to be found in Suffolk and Essex. This use of 'foreign' (that is, not Norfolk) wool and yarn was a complete break with tradition and not achieved without a struggle. When it came to the question of more labour, there was no hope of altering the craft regulations which insisted on seven years' apprenticeship, and restricted the number of apprentices, journeymen and looms that each weaver could have. Nevertheless there were many weavers who disobeyed or evaded the rules, employing journeymen from the countryside, or installing extra looms in country cottages and employing men to work on them there.

It was not merely conservatism which made the authorities insist that all textile workers should be properly trained as apprentices and all employers should be freemen. Much faulty cloth was being produced which threatened to spoil the market for the new materials. But, though most craft guilds were losing their vitality and authority, the Norwich Worsted Weavers' Company, established by Act of Parliament in 1650, proved an exception. The Wardens were given powers to inspect cloth all over the county and to seal those pieces fit for sale; this proved an effective way of maintaining standards.

Thomas Whall, who was Mayor in 1567, thought that too many aliens had settled in the City and made a determined effort to get rid of all of them, but, on the whole, it was felt that the Strangers were profitable and should be encouraged to remain. Similarly, in view of the shortage of skilled labour, the authorities welcomed the boys who came from many parts of England to be apprenticed to Norwich freemen. Most of them came to learn how to make cloth, as worsted weavers, or how to make clothes, as tailors, but there were many other possibilities. During the reign of Elizabeth I apprenticeship to 74 distinct crafts in the City is recorded.

Beggars were a different matter. In about 1570, accor-ding to the Mayor, the City was swarming with tramps and about a fifth of its population was living on charity. A municipal census of this year recorded 2,300 resident poor (as distinct from vagrants) in a total population of about 12,360 persons, but this figure did not include the poor Strangers, who were maintained by their own compatriots. Of the English poor, two-thirds were women, these included many widows and deserted wives. Amongst the men, there were many who were too old to find work easily. There were also many unskilled labourers, ill-paid and frequently unemployed. It is interesting to find in these lists the names of 111 textile workers, additional proof that the native industry had not yet begun to benefit from the introduction of the 'new draperies'. Between 1570 and 1580 the City made vigorous efforts to solve this problem. Begging was forbidden and people who gave to beggars were fined. Tramps were arrested, whipped, and sent back to their places of origin; incomers who might become a burden on the rates were ruthlessly turned out. Meanwhile the inhabitants were made to work. Poor children were apprenticed and women overseers were employed to supervise groups of women and children engaged in spinning and in knitting stockings. Natives found begging or wandering in the streets were committed to the Bridewell. Here they were made to work from 5 a.m. to 8 p.m. with only three-quarters of an hour break – half-an-hour for food and quarter-of-an-hour for prayer. It was assumed that there was work for all able-bodied people; those too young, too old or too ill to labour were maintained out of the rates. For several years after 1570 over £500 a year was disbursed in poor relief, more than the Chamberlains had to spend on ordinary City business.

The plague of 1579 solved the problem for a time. Many of the poor died, and country people avoided the plague-stricken City. But by 1600 the authorities were worried again; the generosity of the merchant class in providing charities and the efficiency with which authorities dealt with the famine of 1597 made the City attractive to the starving rural poor. In this period, as before, Norwich was ruled by a small group of very rich men, many of whom had country estates as well as houses in town. For example Thomas Sotherton, Mayor in 1605, left £8,000 in cash, a very large sum in those days, besides plate and jewels and lands in Swanton, Costessey and Aldenham. But the vast majority of the inhabitants – four-fifths of the whole – were poor or destitute.

The population of Norwich in 1570 was about 12,000, of whom a quarter were aliens. By 1578, the population had increased to just over 16,000, of whom at least 6,000 were aliens. But this growth was drastically checked next year, when about 5,000 people, nearly one-third of the total population, died during an epidemic of bubonic plague. From then until the end of the century, Norwich suffered more severely from the plague than any other provincial town in England and the population never rose much above 11,000.

A Provincial Capital
1642-1815

Between 1671 and 1676 the population of the City was about 21,000; Norwich was then probably the largest provincial town in England. By 1811 the population had risen to 37,256, but by this time some other towns were growing rapidly and Norwich had been surpassed in size by manufacturing centres like Manchester, Birmingham and Leeds, and by ports like Liverpool.

This growth of population in Norwich was partly due to immigration from the countryside, as in former times. By 1800 the cottagers were much worse off than their predecessors had been 50 years before. Agricultural wages in East Anglia were amongst the lowest in England; the cottage industry of hand-spinning was being eroded by the advent of machine-spun yarn from the North. After the war with France began in 1793, food prices soared, and many commons were enclosed for corn lands so that the cottagers lost the fuel and pasture rights they had enjoyed. Many country people came to Norwich seeking work in the worsted industry and many more would have come if the civic authorities had not stopped them. From Tudor times the City had assumed the right to expel people who might become a burden on the rates; in 1662 the right of any Poor Law authority to do this was defined by Statute. Like most industrial cities Norwich tended to allow workers, especially single men, to come in while trade was booming and extra labour was needed, but to turn them out again when a slump came.

The population would have grown faster if towns had been healthier places to live in. Norwich had its last serious epidemic of bubonic plague in 1665-6. According to Blomefield there were 2,251 deaths from plague between 3rd October 1665 and 3rd October 1666, over two-thirds of the total number of deaths. By the summer of 1666 many rich people had fled from the City and most of the shops round the market place were closed. The Town Clerk complained that so many Aldermen had left that it was difficult to govern the City. There was mass unemployment and the weavers could not go into the countryside to work in the harvest as they usually did, because the farmers were afraid to employ them. Money for poor relief was exhausted and there was a real danger that the starving poor would riot, pillage and commandeer empty houses. Fortunately the plague abated as the weather cooled, and a glut of herrings at Yarmouth averted the threat of famine. The Town Clerk wrote on 5th September 1666 that "Twelve herring a penny here fills many an empty bellie".

By 1815 there was more medical care available, even for the poor. The Norfolk and Norwich Hospital, founded in 1771, was the first general hospital of the modern type in Norfolk. By our standards it was primitive in the extreme, with no drains, no piped water, no trained nurses, and only one resident doctor. There were, of course, no antiseptics and no anaesthetics in this or in any other hospital. Yet its importance can hardly be over-estimated, because here, for the first time, the visiting consultants (who all gave their services) became familiar with the diseases of the poor.

From 1642 to 1660 Norwich was depressed, although the City supported the winning side during the Civil War and was outside the battle area. Crushing taxation, which continued through the Commonwealth period, the loss of workers to the forces (Cromwell's famous Maiden Troop was recruited in Norwich), the difficulty of getting yarn from distant parts of England during the Civil War, and the greater difficulty of exporting worsted cloth when ships were being attacked by privateers, all combined to impoverish the citizens. Even after 1660 recovery was retarded by the plague of 1665-6, and by wars. But between 1713 and the outbreak of war with France in 1793, Norwich was probably more prosperous, more influential in its district, and more truly a provincial capital than ever before. This prosperity was largely, though not wholly, due to the expansion of the worsted industry.

After 1713 sales of worsted abroad grew rapidly. Norwich stuffs captured the market from Exeter serges in one European country after the other – Spain, Portugal, Holland and Germany. Her exports to Spain rose from £31,000 in 1711 to £112,000 only ten years later. Norwich stuffs were light, well-finished, attractive in appearance and comparatively cheap to produce because weavers' wages in the City were at times as much as 40% lower than those of comparable workers in the Exeter region. By 1750 Norwich stuffs were going further afield, a great many to the North American colonies until this trade was interrupted by the American War of Independence. The East India Company, which had a monopoly of trade with India and China, ordered quantities of fine camlets. The records of a single Norwich firm (J. & J. Ives and Baseley) for 1791 show them trading in three continents – in Europe with Italy, Spain, Maderia, Germany, Holland, Russia, Norway and Sweden, with Spanish America, and with China. A great deal of worsted fabric was also sold in England and to Ireland, especially in the first half of the century. By 1750 Norwich had developed a wide range of high quality fabrics, some pure worsted (like striped calimancoes) but others made of worsteds and silk (like dorsetteens) or, particularly after 1795, of worsted and cotton. These textiles were attractive, usually brightly col-

28 *Trade token showing a man working at a loom, issued in 1792 by John Harvey, shawl manufacturer of Colegate.*

29 *The Provision market in c.1809. The market has been on this site since the late 11th century.*

oured – Norwich dyeing was of a high standard – and often finished by hotpressing to make them stiff and glossy. Norwich was noted for shawls; the earliest were worsted and hand-embroidered, but these were soon replaced by shawls with complicated patterns woven in various combinations of worsted, silk and cotton. Other textiles made here included coarse stuffs like hempen cloth and sacking, as well as linens, cottons and pure silk.

Norwich was fortunate in that the long fine wool needed for fine worsted all came from the British Isles – chiefly from Lincolnshire though also from Ireland – while the makers of other types of woollen cloth were dependent on supplies from the Continent. There was plenty of hand-spun yarn from East Anglia, the Midlands and Ireland, and, later, at times larger and cheaper supplies of machine-spun yarn from Yorkshire.

Textiles were England's main export in the 18th century and the industry was protected. The export of wool was prohibited; in 1700 the English were forbidden to import printed cotton cloth; between 1720 and 1774 it was illegal to wear it, even if it was made in England. Norwich benefited from these regulations.

Although the industry was generally prosperous during the 18th century, it was not stable; there were many times when there was anxious talk about 'decline' and much distress among the workers. As machine-made cottons captured the home markets Norwich worsted manufacturers became increasingly dependent on their export trade. This always declined in war-time and suffered particularly during the French wars 1793 – 1815, when our traditional markets on the Continent were virtually inaccessible. During these wars the manufacturers came to rely

too much on orders from the East India Company, so that it was a serious blow to them when the Company's Indian monopoly ceased in 1813. The workers suffered greatly from these fluctuations in trade, especially in the Napoleonic Wars when bread was at famine prices.

To the visitor Norwich appeared a city of weavers, but there were other industries, smaller in scope but growing in importance, such as leather-working and brewing. Leather-working had always been important in Norwich and was increasingly so in the 18th century. Herds of cattle fattened on the Yare marshes were driven into the City to be slaughtered, the carcasses going to the butchers' stalls and the hides to the tanners. There was a steady demand in the Norwich region for leather goods, not only for boots and shoes but also for harness and for objects like buckets and hose-pipes which are now made from other materials. Brewers also prospered in 18th century Norwich. There was good water from the chalk and Norfolk grew the best malting barley in the world. Most of the beer was drunk locally and much of the rest was sent to London. By 1801 brewing was big business in Norwich, dominated by half-a-dozen large firms who owned their own maltings and public houses. In that year Patteson's made 20,000 barrels of beer, more than many of the big London firms.

Though Norwich in this period was primarily an industrial city, it was also an important market town and shopping centre for the rural area round it. Parson Woodforde, who was Rector of Weston Longville, about 10 miles away, came into the City to buy his furniture, wine, clothes, etc., and even sent into Norwich for his newspapers and fish.

In this period Norfolk farmers produced more corn and meat than they had done before, so that the food, corn and livestock markets of Norwich were busier than ever,

30 *The Octagon Chapel, Colegate, built for the Presbyterian congregation by Thomas Ivory in 1754 – 6.*

especially after road transport in the 18th century was improved by the making of turnpike roads into the City. When Thomas Baskerville visited Norwich during his tour of England in the reign of Charles II, he said he had never seen so many butchers' stalls. They were open every weekday. By 1780, most of the meat they sold was beef. Joints of pork, veal and lamb were sold by the farmers' wives in another part of the market, together with sausages, dressed poultry, sucking pigs, rabbits, butter, cheese and eggs. The women did not hire stalls, but sat in rows on the cobble-stones with their produce in semi-circular pack baskets or 'peds', and this 'Ped Market' was one of the sights of Norwich. Baskerville also commented on the amount of fish sold; there were as many fish-mongers as butchers. In contrast to today, very little of the food sold in this market was imported, though there were always a few vendors of oranges and lemons.

In the 17th century corn was sold in and around the Market Cross. Baskerville noted sacks of wheat, rye and oats, excellent oatmeal, malt and imported French wheat. In the 18th century corn in Norwich, as in most big markets, was being sold by sample, usually over a drink in an inn, though the City made spasmodic efforts to establish an official corn market in St. Andrew's Hall. Hay could be bought in the Cattle Market as well as in the Haymarket, Norfolk wool in the provision market, other wool in the Guildhall. In May, 1782, William Marshall, who was studying Norfolk farming, made a special journey into Norwich to see the "clover seed market" – clover was an essential part of the Norfolk crop rotation. Marshall was told that the biggest dealer had sold 6½ hundredweight of seed in one afternoon.

The increasing amount of livestock brought in for sale forced the Corporation first to find a new place for the cattle market and then to enlarge and improve it. In 1655 they appointed a committee to inspect the Castle Ditches, which were becoming an unofficial refuse dump; shortly after this the area was in use for stock sales. In 1698 Celia Fiennes noted "a large space for the beast market" under the Castle. In the 18th century the sale area was enlarged by levelling earthworks (1738) and filling in some of the ditches (1774). In 1809 the Corporation provided sheep pens. Communications were improved. In 1792 Rochester

Lane (now Orford Street) was widened, and a road made across the levelled area of the cattle market to King Street. In 1812 the construction of Davey Place – a pedestrian way – linked the provision market with the Castle area.

As early as 1510 the Corporation had attempted to reserve the principal market place for the sale of food; but in spite of this policy and the complaints of shopkeepers, you could buy linen and woollen cloth there in the 1730s, as well as hats, shoes, stockings, clothes of every sort, rope, soap, books and ballads, wooden spoons and spindles from Wymondham, and a host of other things besides.

Before 1750 there were few banks outside London; in the provinces all sorts of people – merchants, manufacturers, tax-collectors, publicans and shop-keepers – acted as unofficial bankers. In 1756, however, Charles Weston opened a bank in Norwich, and there were five others before the end of the century. The most stable and long-lived proved to be that started by the Gurneys in 1775, which still continues as part of Barclays. Many country banks failed because, if there were a sudden panic rush to withdraw deposits, the bank had nothing to draw on but the private fortunes of two or three partners (only the Bank of England was allowed to have shareholders) and dangerously small cash reserves. The Gurneys could weather such storms. John and Henry, who started the bank, had behind them a substantial family fortune made in the worsted trade. Richard Gurney, who joined them in 1779, married the only daughter of David Barclay, who brought her husband great wealth and an invaluable connection with a long-established London bank. As Quakers, they were members of a society whose members were known to be careful and honest in their business dealings and ready to help one another. For all these reasons the Gurneys inspired confidence and attracted custom, and as early as 1781-2 they had established branches at Yarmouth, Lynn, Wisbech and Halesworth at a time when it was very unusual for a country bank to have more than one office.

This period saw the beginning of the insurance business which has become such an important part of the City's economic life. Before 1792 Norwich people insured their lives and property either with London firms like the 'Sun' which had offices in Norwich or, more often, in insurance clubs. A typical advertisement for one of these in 1785 proposes that 60 people should each contribute £1,000, any member whose house was burnt down would receive up to £3,000 and at the end of 30 years the balance would be divided equally amongst the members.

About 1783 Thomas Bignold established himself in Norwich as a wine merchant and banker. In rapid succession he founded the Norwich General Assurance Office (for fire insurance) in 1792, the Norwich Union Fire Insurance Society in 1797 and the Norwich Union Life Insurance Society in 1808. All did well from the start in spite of considerable competition. Success was due to efficient publicity and, in the case of the Life Insurance Society, premiums nearly 20% below those of its most dangerous rival, the Equitable Insurance Company. In order to offer these lower premiums with safety, the Society had to be very careful about the lives it insured and in the first eight years some 500 out of 3,800 proposals were rejected. Most 18th century insurance concerns derived some of their funds from shareholders, but the Norwich Union Societies

31 *Harrison's Wharf, King Street, early 19th century, with wherries and a keel laden with timber.*

were 'fully mutual' – that is, all the capital came from the premiums. Provided that membership was large enough, this was an advantage, because there were no dividends to pay out. The success of the Fire Office showed there was a potential demand for fire insurance facilities from those who could not afford to enter an 'insurance club'. The danger from fire was obvious, not only in the City crowded with old timber-framed houses, but also in the country where there was an added risk of incendiarism, as starving labourers rioted and fired stacks and barns. The Fire Office soon had its own fire brigade and engines, and there were also fire engines belonging to some of the parishes and to the Corporation. In 1742 a building was erected on the Castle Ditches to house the City fire engine and cannon. These fire brigades were often able to stop a small fire from spreading, but, with primitive apparatus and part-time crews, they were helpless in the face of a really big blaze.

The rich worsted manufacturers, brewers and bankers of 18th century Norwich were able to afford expensive imported goods. The East India Company's ships which took Norwich camlets to India and China also brought back tea, porcelain, lacquer panels for the furniture makers, silk fabrics, and wallpaper, amongst other luxuries from China. From North America and the British West Indies came sugar, tobacco, coffee and rum. Cabinet makers from 1660 onwards were making use of costly imported woods for fine furniture, such as French walnut, kingwood from Brazil, satinwood from the East and West Indies, and above all mahogany from the West Indies and the mainland of Central America. A rich Norwich merchant could be expected to have Turkey carpets on his floors, and port, French wines and brandy in his cellar, while his wife's wardrobe might contain Italian velvet, Flemish lace and Indian muslin. These are only a few of the imported luxury goods to be found in 18th century Norwich. Amongst the necessities from overseas were timber and iron from North America and the Baltic countries, though by 1800 most of the needs of the Norwich ironfounders could be met from England.

Many of these commodities came by water. The keels and wherries which sailed from Norwich to Yarmouth carried corn for London and the North and malt for the breweries in London and Holland. They brought back coal from Newcastle and fish from Yarmouth, as well as imported groceries from London and quantities of miscellaneous merchandise from overseas.

From about 1780 the growing number of wheeled vehicles put an increasing strain on the existing road system. Between 1766 and 1823 ten of the main roads leading to the City had been taken over and improved by the Turnpike Trustees, who, because they were allowed to charge tolls, were able to spend more money on road repairs than the parish authorities, who were normally responsible, were able to do. Between 1791 and 1801 all the City gates were taken down on the grounds that they were obstructing traffic, and within the City roads were widened and their surfaces improved, sometimes by the Improvement Commissioners (set up by an Act of 1806) and sometimes by private enterprise. Blackfriars and St. Michael Coslany Bridges were rebuilt and Little Bethel Street and other new roads were constructed. Access from the east was improved when the Enclosure Commissioners made new roads across Mousehold Heath in 1801, and when private companies built the first Foundry and Carrow Bridges, both of which were begun in 1810.

By 1815 the layout of the City had been somewhat modified and its appearance considerably altered. When the gates were removed, the walls were, of course, no longer kept up and there was much more building around and outside them. Parts of the walls fell, as at Ber Street Gate, where a large stretch of wall collapsed in 1807, others were knocked down, and houses built on the site. Alternatively, houses were built up against the wall to save building materials, as in Magpie Road, and some of the towers (long used as dwellings) were converted into cottages. Most of this was slum building, but there were also, by the late 18th century, an increasing number of villas built at Thorpe, Bracondale and Old Catton by business and professional men, who had their offices in the City but their homes outside.

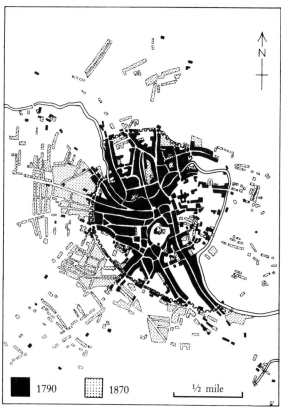

Map 5 *Norwich: built-up area, 1790 and 1870*

1790　　1870　　½ mile

The Changing Scene 1815-1870

The population increased during this period from 37,256 in 1811 to 80,368 in 1871. But whereas Norwich was, in the late 17th century, probably the largest English town after London, by 1861 fifteen provincial towns were larger. People were still coming from the country to settle in Norwich, especially in the parishes outside the walls. The rural workers of East Anglia were desperately poor; a farm labourer's wage in 1815 was 7s. a week and many men were thrown out of work because gangs of women and children were employed on the land at even lower rates. Labourers left the land in such numbers that the population of most Norfolk villages was actually declining by 1850, although the population of England as a whole was increasing by leaps and bounds. But not all the Norfolk migrants came to Norwich. London and the towns of the industrial North were more prosperous and therefore more attractive; indeed many people from the City itself left for these areas, or went overseas.

A detailed report made by a Government Inspector in 1850, after a cholera epidemic, shows that the City was still a very unhealthy place to live in. Some houses had a piped water supply, but this was only available for two or three hours a day on two or three days a week and the water was drawn unfiltered from the filthy river. Poorer people depended on the parish pumps – often situated in churchyards – or on shallow wells. There were no sewers in the modern sense, just overflowing cesspools, or heaps of night soil (one in Worlds End Lane was 9 feet across) which was sold to market gardeners by the cartload. These conditions affected everyone, rich and poor alike, but the rich at least had solid, roomy houses, while those of the poor were damp, dark, dilapidated, overcrowded and verminous. Some of the worst slums were in the old streets, where big houses had become tenements with courts and yards built on what had once been gardens – as in King Street, Magdalen Street and Ber Street. Conditions were equally bad in the low lying districts of Heigham and Pockthorpe and in places like Coburg Street, where houses had been built against the old City walls. Outside the walls new houses had been run up by speculative builders, as at Peafields, New Lakenham, where in 1851 over two thousand people were living without any sanitary provision and with hardly any water. Diseases now rare – typhus, typhoid and diptheria – were then endemic. In 1819 there were 530 deaths from smallpox, nearly all children, and there were epidemics of cholera in 1831 and 1848. Norwich slums were, of course, no worse than those in other towns at the time, and during this period some improvements were made. The old City churchyards, so overcrowded that as early as 1660 they stood high above the road level, were closed after a municipal cemetery had been provided at Bowthorpe in 1855. The new waterworks, begun in 1850, had filtering apparatus and were capable of providing a greater volume of water. A Local Board of Health was set up in 1831 and again in 1851 and, although these committees did not achieve much, they paved the way for the active public health administration which followed the Act of 1870.

By 1870 the built-up area had spread considerably, and much land outside the line of the walls was covered with streets and houses. One reason for this was the coming of the railways. By 1883 Norwich had three terminal stations. All were outside the walls, where it was easier to find large level sites which could be bought at a reasonable price. Railways were constructed by private companies which had no powers of compulsory purchase, so they had to have whatever land they could get at a price they could afford. Thorpe Station, 1844, was built on open meadow land east of the river Wensum. Until 1860 it was reached from Rose Lane, but in this year the construction of Prince of Wales Road provided a better approach. After this, the area round the station was soon built up, with houses for railway workers, hotels for passengers, and factories situated on the banks of the river where they could make use of water transport as well as the railway stations at Thorpe and Trowse. Victoria Station was built just outside St. Stephen's Gate in 1849, utilising the site and some of the buildings of the former Ranelagh Pleasure Gardens. When the Midland and Great Northern Railway Company built the City Station in 1882, on the west bank of the river Wensum just outside Heigham Gate, they provided a new bridge and approach road.

The better-paid artisans were moving out of the courts and yards into new 'artisan suburbs' outside the walls. Hundreds were living in the 'New City' (the Vauxhall Street area) by 1841, while the population of Heigham rose from 842 in 1811 to 5,932 in 1841. At the same time more and more business and professional men were building large houses outside the walled area, as for example along Thorpe Road and on the old City common of Town Close

32 *The original Thorpe Station was built 1843 – 4 as the terminus of the Norwich – Yarmouth line and was linked with London in 1845.*

which was developed as a residential area after 1840.

Yet the City inside the line of the walls was as crowded as ever. Country people moved in to the houses which the artisans had left, and the steep slope from Ber Street to King Street was built up with working-class houses. The new use of cast iron in building construction and the wider introduction of steam power led to the erection of an increasing number of large works and factories, such as the Yarn Company Mill of 1839 at Whitefriars (now Jarrolds printing works) and Bullard's Brewery in Coslany Street of 1868-1874. The workers lived close to these factories. Hours were long and there was no public transport, so that industries could not draw labour from a distance as they do now. Some open places were saved, like Chapel-fields, which became a public park in 1852.

In 1750 worsted weaving was the main industry of Norwich, but by 1901 there was not a single worsted weaver left in the City, though there were about 1,100 workers (mostly women) making silk fabrics and hair cloth. 'Mixed' fabrics had begun to take the place of pure worsted by 1815. Because of the use of machine-spun yarn fewer hands were employed, but the amount of cloth produced and of cash earned was not necessarily much less than before. By 1850 the industry, if not actually contracting, had definitely ceased to grow; other industries were now more important in Norwich, whose textiles, by this time, formed only a tiny proportion of the total British output. Exactly why and when the industry finally declined is a matter of dispute, but it would seem to be the result of interacting causes, none of which, alone, would have proved fatal.

Norwich specialised in high quality fabrics which, until 1840, had to be woven by hand because they were too complicated for machines. But machine-made cloth was cheaper and, in order to avoid being priced out of the

33 *The Norwich Yarn Company's mill, built in 1839. Space in the building was sublet to individual firms and it held 65 spinning frames and 500 power looms.*

market, the Norwich manufacturers had either to reduce quality, which would have exposed them to the full force of competition from Yorkshire machine-made worsted, or cut production costs. They chose the latter course and weavers' wages, always low, were slashed to starvation level. There were riots and strikes, manufacturers' houses were picketed and carriers' carts were wrecked to prevent work being sent to the country weavers whose rates of pay were even lower. These disturbances made it difficult to maintain a high standard of work, especially as it became

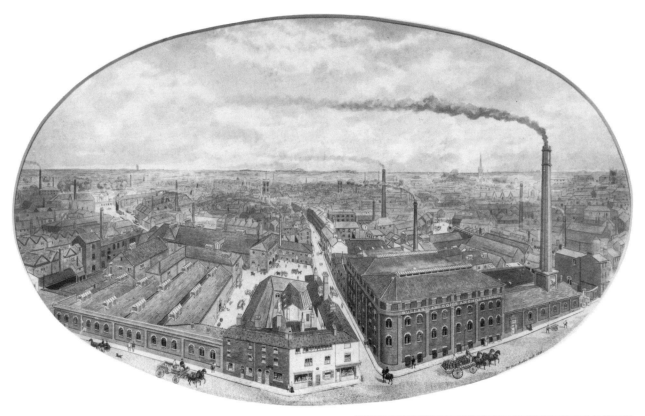

34 *Bullard's Anchor Brewery in the late 19th century. The firm moved to this site in the 1840s.*

increasingly hard to get a steady supply of the long, fine wool used for the best worsteds or worsted mixtures. The old Lincolnshire sheep had been crossed with the New Leicester sheep and the crossbred fleece, though heavier, had shorter and coarser wool. Competition from machine-made textiles, both woollen and cotton, became increasingly fierce after 1833. The Norwich manufacturers themselves installed machines and by 1846 there were 1,700 power looms in the City. But here Norwich was at a disadvantage, it had no swift flowing streams to provide water power and had to import coal from Newcastle for steam-driven machinery. Coal was expensive, the transport cost sometimes exceeding the pit-head price. Costs of transporting wool and finished cloth were also higher than in the Yorkshire worsted area, for Norfolk had no comparable canal system. The Norwich-Lowestoft Navigation, completed in 1833, which made it possible for sea-going ships drawing up to ten feet to reach Norwich, was not the success expected and there were no railways until 1844. After 1850, when the main railway lines from Norwich were completed, the textile trade improved for a time. Also Norwich became an important centre for the distribution of coal brought by rail from the Nottingham-Derby coalfields, though this was to some extent offset by the decline of trade in water-borne coal from Newcastle.

Between 1795 and 1825 silk weaving was a steadier and more lucrative trade than worsted, both for the manufacturer and for the workers, because it was protected. Silk thread was made in Norwich in the early 19th century in

35 *Barnard, Bishop and Barnards' Norfolk Ironworks in Coslany Street. The firm moved here in 1851 and were renowned for their wrought and cast iron products, and wire netting.*

36 *The Sheep Market and Castle in c.1890. The livestock market was held here for about 300 years until 1960 when it was moved to the southern edge of Norwich.*

big mills equipped with powered machinery worked by children. This was cheaper than that imported from the Continent which carried a heavy duty. The import of silk cloth was forbidden altogether until 1815; it is true that a good deal was smuggled in, but this was more difficult after the outbreak of war with France in 1793. After 1838, however, the Norwich industry contracted, because French silks, which came in freely after 1826, were more fashionable, while Manchester silks and machine-made silk-and-cotton fabrics were less costly than Norwich silk-and-worsted ones and very attractive. The industry survived here by specialising in high quality shawls and dress fabrics such as bombazine and challis.

The troubles of the worsted industry were perhaps not so damaging to the City's economy as they appeared to contemporary observers, because other important industries were developing. The boot and shoe trade, for instance, grew slowly but steadily. After 1840 there were boot and shoe manufacturers operating on a big scale and the number of workers increased from 1,913 in 1841, according to the Census, to 6,278 in 1861. By the latter date leather-stitching machinery was in use. The heavy stitching was done by men at home, the closing of the uppers by women and children working in the warehouses of small-scale sub-contractors or 'garret masters'. By 1850 many of the most successful firms were concentrating on women's fashion shoes for export. The brewing industry expanded rapidly between 1800 and 1840 and, though the number of men directly employed was comparatively small, this was probably the most stable and lucrative trade in the City throughout the 19th century.

In the 18th century there had been Norwich soap-boilers who made hard soap for the textile industry out of imported Russian tallow. In 1845 Norwich manufacturers produced over 1½ million pounds of soap, for household as well as industrial use. Paper-making expanded with the establishment of printing works here. Norwich ironfoundries made agricultural implements and steam-engines for Norfolk farmers, miles of wire-netting to help Australian farmers keep out rabbits, and all sorts of domestic hardware and decorative ironwork. In 1854 J. & J. Colman moved from Stoke Holy Cross to Carrow where their new works expanded rapidly, making mustard, flour, blue and starch.

Once the most important railway lines to Norwich had been built, the Norwich corn and livestock markets prospered at the expense of those in nearby places like Wymondham and Hingham. A Corn Exchange was provided in 1825, not by the Corporation but by a private company. Great numbers of Irish store cattle came by rail to Trowse Station and were sold on the Castle hill; in the 12 months ending June 1867, 57,058 came into Trowse Station and 35,083 went out. The banks which served the farmers expanded their business, but the local insurance business was stagnant, if not actually declining.

In this period, overseas trade flourished. The developing British colonies of India, South Africa, Canada, Australia and New Zealand provided a good market for Norwich-made agricultural machinery, general hardware, shoes and wire netting. Textiles continued to be exported although not in such great quantities as earlier in the 19th century. A huge variety of raw materials were imported from all over the world for use in local manufacturing industry and Norwich merchants were dealing in imported timber, groceries, wines and spirits, guano and gutta-percha.

37 *The Guildhall and Market Place in 1914, showing the tramline opened in 1900 and the Fish Market built 1857 – 60.*

The Modern City
1870-1980

The census of 1871 gave the population of Norwich as 80,386; by 1911 this had increased to 121,490. In 1921, however, the figure was only 120,661. This did not mean that the population of the settlement had diminished, but that the built-up area had spread beyond the legal boundary. In fact, the population of the whole built-up area, estimated in 1980 at 180,000, has grown slowly but steadily throughout this period. Some of this growth was due to the natural increase of the population in an environment healthier than in the past. In 1873 the death rate was 21 per thousand, in 1970 the crude death rate was 12.6 per thousand, though for Norwich, as for England as a whole, the effects of this have been offset to some extent by a fall in the birth rate. The population in 1971 was 121,688.

Norwich is now a healthier place to live in than ever before because of the revolution in public health administration and medical care since 1870. The City appointed its first Medical Officer of Health in 1875. At that time smallpox was still a common disease here, typhoid was endemic (there were 98 deaths in 1898) and tuberculosis was rampant. Epidemics swept through the slums, for the Corporation had no isolation hospital and could do nothing to improve the condition of the courts and yards, which were private property. But the authorities did at least realise the connection between dirt and disease. They began to lay the first sewer in 1869; in 1877 they embarked on their first slum clearance scheme and in 1889 acquired powers to compel the owners of courts and yards to

drain, level and pave them. Progress was slow, for the City was not prosperous and money for these projects was difficult to find – the sewerage scheme was bitterly attacked on the score of expense. In 1910 living conditions were still very bad in the poorer parts of the City, and very high death rates were recorded in New Lakenham, Hellesdon, Heigham and Pockthorpe. After World War I, however, the Corporation embarked on the great programme of slum clearance and rehousing which has gone on ever since.

Some of the increase of population was due, as in former times, to immigration. By 1875 English agriculture was deeply depressed and one-tenth of Norfolk farm labourers had left the land by 1891. Many came to Norwich where a labourer could earn 16s to 21s. a week instead of 10s. on a farm, where his women folk had more chance of employment, and where there were more houses. Modern Norwich also has its 'Strangers'; many foreigners, including refugees, have come here, some to settle permanently, others to work or to study for only a short time. Hundreds of people who come into the City to work from as far as Wells and Watton help to swell the daytime population of the City, which offers a wide range of employment in factories and offices and in shops which serve a wide rural hinterland.

During the last 100 years, the City has changed more in appearance than ever before. The built-up area has spread far beyond the City boundary. Not only has the population increased in size, but housing standards have risen, so that a thousand people living in Norwich today occupy much more space than at any time in the past. The advent of public transport and the car made it possible for far more people to live at a distance from their work. There was an acute housing shortage everywhere after World War I, and a great many new houses were built along the main roads leading out of the City or on land made available by the break up of country estates due to heavy taxation and agricultural depression. New Costessey began as a shack town of wooden huts, railway carriages and mud tracks on the land which the Jerninghams sold in 1918. It is outside the City boundary but is an extension of the built-up area. Moreover, since 1918 the authorities have been re-housing people from the centre of the City in big municipal estates on the outskirts, where acres of land might be needed to accommodate the inhabitants of a few overcrowded courts. New schools have been built to cater for the children on these estates and these, with their specialised classrooms and playing fields, occupy far more space than did their predecessors, the Board Schools of 1870. For example, at Lakenham 56 acres are needed to accommodate two modern schools; the University of East Anglia began building in 1963 on a 272 acre site to the west of the City and now has over 4,000 students.

Modern industry, like modern education, occupies a lot of space. The big works and mills built inside the City in the 19th century were often several storeys high, but in most modern factories all the machinery is on ground level, and so arranged that the product can be moved quickly and easily from one place to the next. May and Baker Ltd., a chemical firm which came to the City in 1958, acquired a 180 acre site to allow for this kind of layout and for future expansion.

As a result of the flight to the fringe, some residential districts near the centre came to have a depressed appearance. Some were 19th century artisan suburbs, like the 'New City', which had streets of small terraced houses, corner shops, and public houses. Others, like Surrey Street and All Saints Green, had been 'good' residential areas, with big houses which are now split up into offices and flats. During the last fifteen years, much has been done to give new life to the inner-city area. An ambitious conservation programme combining the modernisation of many houses and artisans' cottages, together with selective rebuilding in the vernacular style has revitalised parts of the City such as Norwich Over-the-Water and Pottergate, thereby checking the drift of population to the outskirts. Other schemes have been concerned with the rejuvenation of run-down shopping streets and the success of these has greatly enlivened the commercial face of the City.

During World War II, Norwich suffered severely from enemy bombing. Over 3,000 houses were damaged, 2,000 of them beyond repair. A number of churches were destroyed and some of them, including St. Michael at Thorn and St. Benedict, have not been rebuilt, because there are now far more churches in the centre of the City than are needed for the small population that still lives there. Some of the redundant churches which are still intact have been turned to other uses; for example the church of St. Peter Hungate is now a museum of church art. City Station was put out of action for a time, as was the Goods Station at Norwich Thorpe. Many shops were

38 *Bull's Head Yard off Ber Street. Norwich had over 700 small courts and yards in the late 19th century, many of them appalling slums.*

39 *The City's conservation programme has led to the restoration of many old houses, such as these around a medieval courtyard off Duke Street.*

40 *The recent policy to build new housing in the inner city has resulted in ambitious developments such as Barnard's Yard off Colegate, completed in 1979.*

41 *The Caley Mackintosh factory in Chapelfield Road was destroyed by fire following an air-raid during the night of 29th April, 1942.*

destroyed and over 100 factories. When it came to rebuilding, some firms chose to put up a new factory on their old site, as did John Mackintosh & Sons Ltd. in Chapelfield and Morgans Brewery on King Street, but others, like F. W. Harmer & Co., decided to move from cramped sites in the centre to more spacious ones on the outskirts.

The impact of the car on the appearance of Norwich has been profound. In spite of a complicated one-way system, traffic congestion in the centre continues and large areas have had to be reserved for car parks. Indeed, the entire Medieval street pattern is threatened by the need to provide for an ever-increasing volume of motor traffic; in 1962-4, for instance, an important Medieval thoroughfare, St. Stephens Street, had to be widened and parts of the ancient street plan in the area of the walled City north of the river have been obliterated by new building. However, the new Inner Ring Road has helped to preserve the heart of the City by easing the pressure of traffic at the centre. Meanwhile, the conversion of a number of central streets – London Street, Dove Street, Lower Goat Lane and White Lion Street – into walkways which are closed to vehicles, has provided a welcome refuge for sightseers and shoppers alike.

Norwich now has a thriving civil airport, built on part of the former R.A.F. airfield at Horsham St. Faiths, with regular flights to other British cities and major Continental centres. Rail transport, on the other hand, has deteriorated; Norwich had three passenger stations in 1890 but has only one now and even on the surviving passenger lines there are fewer trains. The trade of the Port of Norwich, which increased after World War II, has contracted

since the mid 1960s. Until then, coal was brought by river for the gas works and electricity generating station. Now, with North Sea gas and a new oil-fired power station, only a handful of firms use the river for commercial trade although it is increasingly used by pleasure craft.

In the 20th century there has been much more building by public authorities than ever before in the City's history. The great housing estates, which have shops and schools as well as houses, have already been mentioned. A new City Hall was completed in 1938; the market place was enlarged and Bethel Street widened at the same time. The new Public Library, erected on an adjacent site was opened in 1963 and new Law Courts are being built on the former Gas Works site at Whitefriars. Norwich's most radical piece of modern architecture, the Sainsbury Centre, on the University campus, was built in 1978 to house the art collections of Sir Robert and Lady Sainsbury. In order to economise on site space some very lofty public and commercial buildings have been erected, such as the blocks of the Norfolk and Norwich Hospital, opened in 1968. There is today much more public control of building than formerly. In 1870, for example, an industrialist could build his factory wherever he chose, provided he could buy the land he wanted. Now, the location of factories and offices is controlled both by central government and the local planning authority. In Norwich, for example, most recent factories have been built on sites near the Outer Ring Road, in accordance with the City's planning policy, whilst H.M. Stationery Office has been installed in new premises in Botolph Street as part of a Government plan to move some of its offices out of London.

The modern industrial scene is very varied. There are trades with a long history, like shoemaking, and there are some which have only recently come to the City, like the manufacture of weed killers and insecticides. For Norwich, where building costs are rather lower and labour rather easier to find than in some intensely industrialised areas, has recently attracted several new industries, especially since the ban on new factories in the London area. Some Norwich firms such as F. W. Harmer & Co. Ltd. make large quantities of standardised products like military uniforms. Others specialise in the making of goods, including machinery, to order. There is heavy industry, such as engineering and ironfounding, which employs mostly men, and light industry, like the manufacture of chocolate and crackers, which employs mostly women. Among the specialised products of Norwich are paint tins, plastic bottles and electric switches. The most important industries in terms of the number of people employed are clothing (which includes shoe-making), building construction, the manufacture of food and drink, engineering and printing.

In 1870 the manufacture of boots and shoes was largely in the hands of small employers, or 'garret masters'. Many of the processes were carried out by workers in their own homes but now almost all production takes place within the factory walls. In 1870 there was little machinery in use except the sewing machine but after the strike of 1897 a few of the bigger employers began to install machinery imported from America. Now new devices are making it possible for fewer workers to produce more shoes. Norwich has long specialised in the manufacture of high quality women's fashion shoes and children's footwear. In spite of the difficult conditions affecting the industry nationally,

42 *The City Hall, designed by C. H. James and S. R. Pierce, was opened in 1938. The photograph (1956) shows the south side of Bethel Street before redevelopment.*

some 4,500 people are employed here, making around 5½ million pairs of shoes annually. In 1870 there were a great many tailors and dressmakers making clothes to measure for individual customers. There are few now, for most people buy ready-made clothes. Men's clothing, including uniforms, has been manufactured in Norwich since 1820.

The building trade has experienced considerable fluctuations during the last hundred years. The boom at the turn of the century when the sewers were being reconstructed, tram-lines laid and streets widened, was followed by a slump and much unemployment among building workers. After the first World War there was a great deal of house-building, both public and private, and again until recently, constructional work of every kind – new roads, schools, shops and office blocks – ensured employment for building workers and demolition men. Latterly, however, the national economic recession has curbed public and private development.

When the sociologist Hawkins described the industries of Norwich in 1910, he regarded engineering and iron-founding as declining industries, except for the manufacture of electric motors, which had begun in 1880. In 1980, the largest single employer in manufacturing industry was an engineering firm, Laurence Scott & Electromotors Ltd. Some of the products of Norwich engineers go all over the globe, such as wire-netting, packing machinery, heating plant, control gear for ships and nuclear submarines, and some of the world's largest electric motors. Norwich engineering firms have taken part in the search for oil and gas below the North Sea.

Changes have also taken place in the food and drink

industries. In 1870, milling was still important and Norwich had a number of small wind and watermills grinding locally grown wheat. But by 1900, most of the grain used in England was imported and ground at the ports. One mill, Read Woodrow Ltd., has survived to the present day and still produces flour from locally grown and imported wheat. The two major companies manufacturing foodstuffs are Colman Foods, making mustard, cereals, baby foods and soft drinks, and Rowntree Mackintosh Ltd. making chocolate and confectionery.

Since the mid 19th century, there has been an increasing tendency for brewing to be concentrated in the hands of a few large firms. By 1930 there were four big breweries in the City but now, because of closure and take-over, only the Norwich Brewery Ltd. remains. In 1870 a chemist called Caley was making mineral water as a sideline; today this is an important industry due to the constant demand for soft drinks. Norwich has long had its jobbing printers and its local newspapers. The *Norwich Post* was the first provincial paper and today, several, newspapers are still published in the City including the *Eastern Daily Press*, one of the few remaining provincial dailies. During the 19th century, the scope of the general printing trade was enlarged, so that by 1900 a good deal of work was being done here for London and other places outside East Anglia, Today printing of every kind is undertaken in the City and high quality colour printing is a speciality.

In 1870 the local insurance business was stagnating but, after John Deuchar became General Manager of the Norwich Union Life Office in 1887, agencies were set up in most countries in Europe and in many place in the

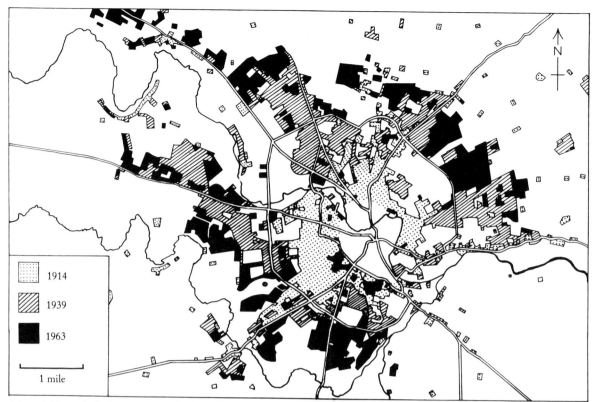

Map 6 *Norwich: built-up area outside the walls, 1914, 1939 and 1963*

Commonwealth. Today, Norwich Union is one of the biggest insurance companies in the country and the largest employer in the City.

Norwich has more shops and more banks than most towns of its size because it serves a very large rural hinterland. The provision market is busier than it was twenty years ago, but there is much less local produce sold than was formerly the case. The livestock market was affected by the agricultural depressions at the end of the 19th century and after World War I, but not so badly as the rural markets; what trade remained came to Norwich. Since the beginning of World War II in 1939, Norfolk farming has generally prospered and the market prospered too, till the old-fasioned market place and its approaches became intolerably congested on market days. In July 1960, a new livestock market on a 32 acre site was opened near the City boundary at Harford. The old market place is now used as a car park except at fair times.

As a result of the 1964-5 Boundary Commission, the County Borough area was extended only slightly, excluding many of the suburbs such as Thorpe. To the north most of the area of Norwich Airport came into the city, while to the west an area of farmland containing the deserted village of Bowthorpe was taken in. This has been built up as both a residential and industrial area, some development being carried out by the Local Authority and the rest by private enterprise. The reoganisation of Local Government in 1974 brought no change to the city boundaries but Norwich lost its County Borough status, becoming a District Council. This resulted in the loss of a number of its powers to the County Council.

The 20th century has seen more dramatic changes in Norwich than any other period. Change will inevitably continue but the experience of previous development has contributed to a greater sensitivity towards the past than has been seen before. The designation of Conservation Areas has led to a sustained effort to preserve and restore many of the older parts of the City and to ensure that new building is, as far as possible, in keeping with the existing architecture. The unique character of Norwich derives from its diversity; from the survival of houses, churches, and public and industrial buildings of all periods. It is in the Norwich which we have today that the growth of the City, which started over a thousand years ago, is demonstrated.

Bibliography

This brief and selective bibliography lists only a few of the books, pamphlets and manuscripts relating to Norwich; many others are available in the Local Studies Department of the Norwich Central Library and in the Norfolk Record Office.

Archaeological Excavations

HURST, J. G. and GOLSON, J. (1957) Excavations at St. Benedict's Gates, Norwich, 1951 and 1953. *Norf. Arch.*, 31, pp. 5 – 112.

HURST, J. G. (1963) Excavations at Barn Road, Norwich, 1954 – 5. *Norf. Arch.*, 33, Pt. II, pp. 131 – 179.

JOPE, E. M. (1948) Excavations in the city of Norwich. *Norf. Arch.*, 30, pp. 287 – 323.

NORFOLK ARCHAEOLOGICAL UNIT — reports of excavations 1979 onwards will be published in forthcoming volumes of *East Anglian Archaeology*.

NORWICH SURVEY — interim reports of excavations 1971 – 1978 are published annually in *Norf. Arch.* vols. 35 – 37, 1972 – 1978. Final reports will be published in forthcoming volumes of *East Anglian Archaeology*.

Historical and general studies

ALLEN, B. E. (1951) *The administrative and social structure of the Norwich merchant class 1484 – 1660.* (University of Havard. Unpublished PhD. thesis. Copy in Norwich Public Library).

ALLISON, K. J. (1955) *The Wool supply and the worsted cloth industry in Norfolk in the 16th and 17th centuries.* (University of Leeds, unpublished thesis. Copy in Norwich Public Library).
(1960) The Norfolk Worsted Industry Pt.1. The Traditional Industry. *Yorks, Bull. of Econ. and Soc. Research*, 12, no. 2, pp. 73 – 83.
(1961) The Norfolk Worsted Industry Pt.2. The Norfolk Worsted Industry in the 16th and 17th centuries. *Ibid*, 13, no. 2, pp. 61-77.

ANDERSON, D. S. (1959) *Norwich: a study in urban geography.* (University of London. Unpublished M.Sc. thesis. Copy in Norwich Public Library).

ASSISTANT HAND-LOOM WEAVERS' COMMISSIONERS (1839) *Reports*, 1, pp. 335 – 350. London.

BANGER, J. (1974) *Norwich at War.* Norwich

BAYNE, A. D. (1858) *An Account of the Industry and Trade of Norwich and Norfolk.* 2nd ed. Norwich.

BIDWELL, W. H. (1900) *Annals of an East Anglian Bank.* Norwich.

BLAKE, P. W., BULL, J., CARTWRIGHT, A. R. and FITCH, A. (revised ed. 1969) *The Norfolk we live in.* Norwich.

BLAKE, R. (1958) *Esto Perpetua: Norwich Union Life Insurance Society 1808 – 1958.* London.

BLAKELY, E. T. *History of the manufacturers of Norwich.* (no date, written between 1842 and 1851).

BLOMEFIELD, F. (1805 – 10) *Essay towards a topographical history of the country of Norfolk*, vols. 3 – 4, 2nd ed. Norwich.

BRITISH ASSOCIATION FOR THE ADVANCEMENT OF SCIENCE (1935) *A scientific survey of Norwich and district.* London.
(1961) *Norwich and its Region.* Norwich.

BUCHANAN, C. (1963) *Traffic in Towns*, pp. 112 – 123. London.

BURGESS, E., and W. L. (1904) *Men Who Have Made Norwich.* Norwich.

CAMPBELL, J. (1975) *Norwich* (Atlas of Historic Towns fascicle. London.

CARTER, A. (1978) "The Anglo-Saxon Origins of Norwich: the problems and approaches". *Anglo-Saxon England*, vol. 7, pp. 175 – 204. Cambridge.

CLABBURN, P. (1975) *Norwich Shawls.* Norwich.

CLAYTON, E. G. (1980) *The First 100 Years of Telephones Viewed from Norwich.* Norwich.

COLVIN, H. M. (1963) *A History of the King's Works*, vol. I, pp. 753 – 755 (Norwich Castle). London.

COMMISSIONERS ON MUNICIPAL CORPORATIONS IN ENGLAND AND WALES (1835) *Report on the Corporation of Norwich.* London.

CORFIELD, P. J. (1972) "A provincial capital in the late seventeenth century: The case of Norwich". from P. Clark and P. Slack, eds., *Crisis and Order in English Towns*, pp. 263 – 310. London.
(1980) *Towns, trade, religion and radicalism: The Norwich perspecitve on English History.* Norwich.

COZENS-HARDY, B. and KENT, E. A. (1938) *The Mayors of Norwich 1403 – 1855.* Norwich and London.

DAY, M. (1977) *Brewing in Norwich.* Norwich.

DOW, G. (1947) *The first railway in Norfolk.* 2nd ed. London.

DRAKE, G. R. (1967) *Bubonic plague in Norwich in the late 16th and early 17th centuries.* (Unpublished thesis. Copy in Norwich Public Library).

DUNN, I. and SUTERMEISTER, H. (c. 1975) *The Norwich Guildhall*, Norwich. (not dated).

EDWARDS, J. K. (1963) *The economic development of Norwich with particular reference to the worsted industry.* (University of Leeds, unpublished thesis. Copy in Norwich Public Library).
(1963) The Gurneys and the Norwich Clothing Trade in the Eighteenth Century. *The Journal of the Friends' Historical Society*, vol. 50, no. 3, pp. 134 – 152.
(1964) The Decline of the Norwich Textiles Industry. *Yorkshire Bulletin of Economic and Social Research*, vol. 16, no. 1, pp. 31 – 41.
(1967) Chartism in Norwich. *Ibid*, vol. 19, no. 2, pp. 85 – 100.

EVANS, J. T. (1979) *Seventeenth Century Norwich Politics, Religion and Government 1620 – 1690.* Oxford.

ed. EWING, W. C. (1850) *Notices and illustrations of the costume processions, pageantry etc. formerly displayed by the Corporation of Norwich.* Norwich.

HEIDENSTAM, D. (1962) *The port of Norwich: a survey of its seaborne trade 1949 – 1961.* (Unpublished thesis. Copy in Norwich Public Library).

HUDSON, W. (1896) *How the city of Norwich grew into shape.* Norwich.

HUDSON, W. and TINGEY, J. C. (1906 − 10) *Records of the city of Norwich.* Norwich.

INSTITUTE OF GEOLOGICAL SCIENCES (in press) *Geological Memoir, Norwich Sheet.* London.

JEWSON, C. B. (1975) *The Jacobin City. A Portrait of Norwich in its Reaction to the French Revolution 1788 − 1802.* Glasgow and London.

KENNETT, D. H. (1971) 'Mayor-making at Norwich', *Norfolk Archaeology,* 35, pt. II, pp. 271 − 3.

KETTON-CREMER, R. W. (1957) The Coming of the Strangers. *Norfolk Assembly,* pp. 113 − 130. London.

KIRKPATRICK, J. (1845) *History of the religious orders and communities, and of the hospitals and castle of Norwich, written about the year 1725.* (ed. Dawson Turner). Norwich.
(1889) *Streets and Lanes of the City of Norwich.* (ed. W. Hudson). Norwich.

LAND, S. K. (1977) *Kett's Rebellion. The Norfolk Rising of 1549.* Ipswich.

LEE, W. (1850) *Report to the General Board of Health on a preliminary enquiry into the sewerage, drainage, and supply of water, and the sanitary condition of the inhabitants of Norwich.* Norwich.

LIPMAN, V. D. (1967) *The Jews of Medieval Norwich.* London.

ed. MACKIE, C. (1901) *Norfolk Annals 1801 − 1900.* Norwich.

MAXWELL, R. I. and WOOD, A. A. (1966) *City of Norwich and County of Norfolk: a joint growth study.* Norwich.

ed. MILLICAN, P. (1934) *The Register of the Freemen of Norwich 1548 − 1713.* Norwich.
(1952) *The Freemen of Norwich 1714 − 1752.* (Norfolk Record Society, vo. 23). Norwich.

MOENS, W. J. C. (1887 − 1832) *The Walloons and their church at Norwich: their history and registers 1565 − 1832.* (Publications of the Huguenot Society of London, vol. I). Lymington.

MUNCASTER, M. J. (1969) *The 19th century epidemics of cholera in Norwich and Norfolk.* (University of East Anglia. Unpublished M.A. thesis. Copy in Norwich Public Library).

NORWICH COUNTY BOROUGH COUNCIL (1945) *City of Norwich Plan.* Norwich.
(1967) *Draft Urban Plan.* Norwich.

PAGE, R. and PALGRAVE-MOORE, P. (1975) *Census of Norwich 1851 Part 1: St. Martin at Palace and St. Martin at Oak.* (Norfolk Genealogy, vol. VII, Norfolk and Norwich Genealogical Society). Norwich.

PALGRAVE-MOORE, P. (1978) *The Mayors and Lord Mayors of Norwich 1836 − 1974.* Norwich.

PEVSNER, N. (1962) *The Buildings of England: North-East Norfolk and Norwich.* pp. 204 − 293. Harmondsworth.

POUND, J. F. (1960) *Norwich public health 1845 − 80.* (University of Birmingham, unpublished thesis. Copy in Norwich Public Library).
(1962) *The Elizabethan Corporation of Norwich 1558 − 1603.* (University of Birmingham, unpublished thesis).
(1962) An Elizabethan census of the poor: the treatment of vagrancy in Norwich 1570 − 80. *Birmingham Hist. Journ.,* vol. 8, no. 2.
(1966) The social and trade structure of Norwich 1525 − 1575. *Past and Present,* July 1966.
(1968) *The social structure and governing classes of Norwich 1525 − 1675.* (unpublished article).
(1972) *The Norwich census of the poor 1570.* (Norfolk Record Society, vol. 40). Norwich.

(1975) Government and Society in Tudor and Stuart Norwich 1525 − 1675. (University of Leicester, unpublished thesis. Copy in Norwich Public Library).

RICKWOOD, D. (1967) *The origin and decline of the Stranger community of Norwich, with special reference to the Dutch Congregation 1565 − 1706.* (University of East Anglia. Unpublished M.A. thesis. Copy in Norwich Public Library).

ed. RISING, W. M. and MILLICAN, P. (1959) *An index of indentures of Norwich apprentices enrolled with the Norwich Assembly Henry VII − George II.* (Norfolk Record Society, vol. 29). Norwich.

ROYAL ARCHAEOLOGICAL INSTITUTE (1951) Report of the Summer Meeting at Norwich 1949. *Arch. Journ.,* 106, pp. 74 − 98.
(1979) Programme of the Summer Meeting at Norwich 1979.

RUDD, W. R. (1923) The Norfolk and Norwich Silk Industry. *Norf. Arch.,* 21, pp. 245 − 282.

RYE, W. (1877) The Dutch Refugees in Norwich. *Norfolk Antiquarian Miscellany,* vol. 3, pp. 185 − 248. Norwich.
(1917) *History of the parish of Earlham.* Norwich.
(1917) *History of the parish of Eaton.* Norwich.
(1917) *History of the parish of Heigham.* Norwich.
(1917) *History of the parish of Hellesdon.* Norwich.
(1919) *History of the parish of Catton.* Norwich.

ed. RYE, W. (1888) *Calendar of the freemen of Norwich from 1317 to 1603 compiled by John L'Estrange.* London.

ed. SACHSE, W. L. (1942) *Minutes of the Norwich Court of Mayoralty 1630 − 1.* Norfolk Record Society, vol. 15). Norwich.
(1967) *Minutes of the Norwich Court of Mayoralty 1632 − 3.* (Ibid, vol. 36). Norwich

ed. SAUNDERS, H. W. (1939) *The first register of Norwich Cathedral Priory.* (Norfolk Record Society, vol. 11). Norwich.

SPARKES, W. (1949) *Shoemaking in Norwich.* Norwich.

SUSSEX, V. J. (1980) *The Norwich Post Office 1568 − 1980.* Coggeshall.

SUTERMEISTER, H. (1977) *The Norwich Blackfriars.* Norwich.

TAYLOR, R. (1821) *Index Monasticus or the abbeys and other monasteries . . . formerly established in the Diocese of Norwich and the ancient Kingdom of East Anglia.* London.

THURLOW, G. (1972) *Norwich Cathedral.* Norwich.

TILLETT, N. R. (1950) *How Norwich is governed.* Norwich.

TRAMWAY AND OMNIBUS HISTORICAL SOCIETY (1960) *The Norwich Tramways 1900−1935.* Norwich.

VARIOUS AUTHORS (1926) An industrial survey of Norwich. *Manchester Guardian Commercial,* Feb. 11, vol. 21, no. 297.
(1958) Industry 1958. *Eastern Daily Press,* March 18, supplement.
(1963) Industry 1963. *Eastern Daily Press,* March 3, supplement.
(1967) Industry 1967. *Eastern Daily Press,* May 10, supplement.

WOODWARD, H. B. (1881) *The Geology of the country around Norwich.* (Memoirs of the Geological Survey of England and Wales). London.

Directories before 1914

Norwich
  W. Chase 1783
  T. Peck 1802
  C. Berry 1810
  G. Blyth 1842
  Mason 1852
  Roger 1859
  Simpson 1864
  Mathieson 1867
  Colman 1877
  Hamilton 1879
  Eyre 1883
  Jarrold 1886, 1889, 1894, 1900, 1905, 1911, 1913
Norfolk
  W. White 1836, 1845, 1854 (Francis White) 1864, 1883,
  1890
  Kelly 1853, 1858, 1865, 1875, 1879, 1883, 1888, 1892,
  1900, 1904, 1908, 1910, 1912
National
  Universal British 1793
  Pigot 1823, 1830, 1840
  Robson 1839
  Kelly 1846
  Slater 1850

Norwich Bibliographies

CHUBB, T. and STEPHEN, G. A. (1928) *A descriptive list
of the printed maps of Norfolk 1574 — 1916 and a descriptive list
of Norwich plans 1541 — 1914.* Norwich.

DARROCH, E. and TAYLOR, B. ed. (1975) *A Bibliography of
Norfolk History.* Norwich.

RYE, W. (1881) *An index to Norfolk topography.* London.
(1924) *A Handbook to the Materials available to Students of
Local History and Genealogy, arranged in order of date.* (Norfolk
Handbooks, New Series no. 1). Norwich.

STEPHEN, G. A. (1919) *Guide to the Study of Norwich.* 2nd ed.
Norwich.